First World War
and Army of Occupation
War Diary
France, Belgium and Germany

59 DIVISION
177 Infantry Brigade,
Brigade Trench Mortar Battery
1 March 1917 - 31 December 1918

WO95/3023/8

The Naval & Military Press Ltd
www.nmarchive.com
Published in association with The National Archives

Published by

The Naval & Military Press Ltd

Unit 10 Ridgewood Industrial Park,
Uckfield, East Sussex,
TN22 5QE England
Tel: +44 (0) 1825 749494

www.naval-military-press.com

www.nmarchive.com

This diary has been reprinted in facsimile from the original. Any imperfections are inevitably reproduced and the quality may fall short of modern type and cartographic standards.

© **Crown Copyright**
Images reproduced by permission of The National Archives, London, England, 2015.

Contents

Document type	Place/Title	Date From	Date To
Heading	WO95/3023/9 Brigade Trench Mortar Battery		
Heading	59th Division 177th Infy Bde Trench Mortar Bty Apr. 1917-Dec. 1918.		
War Diary	Bavon-Vilers	01/03/1917	03/03/1917
War Diary	Foucaucourt	04/03/1917	04/03/1917
War Diary	Belloy	05/03/1917	20/03/1917
War Diary	Foucaucourt	21/03/1917	31/03/1917
War Diary	Vaux-Armenois	01/04/1917	08/04/1917
War Diary	Hamelet	09/04/1917	11/04/1917
War Diary	Hesbecourt	12/04/1917	18/04/1917
War Diary	Flechin	19/04/1917	30/04/1917
Heading	War Diary Of This Unit For Month Of May		
War Diary	Sugar Factory Montigny Farm	01/05/1917	14/05/1917
War Diary	Vraignes	15/05/1917	24/05/1917
War Diary	L.10.a. Central	26/05/1917	31/05/1917
War Diary	L 10 A 4.5	01/06/1917	16/06/1917
War Diary	Q28C 2.4	17/06/1917	21/06/1917
War Diary	V10 65.3	22/06/1917	27/06/1917
War Diary	Equancourt	28/06/1917	28/06/1917
War Diary	V 10 65.3	28/06/1917	30/06/1917
War Diary	V.10.F.5.3	01/07/1917	01/07/1917
War Diary	Q20 A-1-1.	02/07/1917	09/07/1917
War Diary	O.16-Central	10/07/1917	31/07/1917
Operation(al) Order(s)	Operation Order No. 4.	22/07/1917	22/07/1917
Operation(al) Order(s)	177th Eight French Motar Battery Operation Order No:- 6		
War Diary	O.16-Central	01/08/1917	22/08/1917
War Diary	Senlis (P.10.d.5.8).	23/08/1917	30/08/1917
War Diary	Winnezeele (J.10.a-8.6)	31/08/1917	19/09/1917
War Diary	Luna Park	20/09/1917	22/09/1917
War Diary	Socalfrch Clateace	23/09/1917	23/09/1917
War Diary	Wieltje	24/09/1917	30/09/1917
War Diary	Vlamertinghe (No. 2 Area)	01/10/1917	01/10/1917
War Diary	2.J-2-3	02/10/1917	02/10/1917
War Diary	Hamet Billet	03/10/1917	05/10/1917
War Diary	Erny St. Julien	06/10/1917	09/10/1917
War Diary	Bdurs	10/10/1917	10/10/1917
War Diary	Maisnil Le Ruitz	11/10/1917	11/10/1917
War Diary	Vancouver Camp	12/10/1917	12/10/1917
War Diary	Avion	13/10/1917	16/10/1917
War Diary	N.31-C.9-1	17/10/1917	21/10/1917
War Diary	Gouy Servins Q.35.d.0.6.	22/10/1917	28/10/1917
War Diary	M.23-D-1-9	29/10/1917	31/10/1917
War Diary	M.23.b-05.2	01/11/1917	10/11/1917
War Diary	M-23.b.0-5	11/11/1917	11/11/1917
War Diary	M-23.b.5-2	12/11/1917	14/11/1917
War Diary	Q.35-D.0.6.	15/11/1917	16/11/1917
War Diary	J.35-C-5-0	17/11/1917	18/11/1917
War Diary	W.2-C.5.0	19/11/1917	20/11/1917
War Diary	G.13.b.8.7	21/11/1917	21/11/1917

Type	Location	Start	End
War Diary	W.2.C.5.0.	22/11/1917	26/11/1917
War Diary	L.13-C.1-3.	27/11/1917	14/12/1917
War Diary	K.29.d-1-6	15/12/1917	16/12/1917
War Diary	Flesquires	17/12/1917	22/12/1917
War Diary	Havrincourt	23/12/1917	23/12/1917
War Diary	Rocquigny	24/12/1917	24/12/1917
War Diary	Ambrines	25/12/1917	31/12/1917
War Diary	Ambrines I.3.C.O.5.	01/02/1918	08/02/1918
War Diary	P.24 B.2.7.	09/02/1918	09/02/1918
War Diary	X.10.b.4.8.	10/02/1918	10/02/1918
War Diary	A.5.b.45.25.	11/02/1918	11/02/1918
War Diary	B 17.b.5.5.	12/02/1918	28/02/1918
Miscellaneous	Headquarters 59 Division	11/04/1918	11/04/1918
War Diary	B.17.b.5.5	01/03/1918	10/03/1918
War Diary	C.8.a.25-15.	11/03/1918	19/03/1918
War Diary	Mory	20/03/1918	22/03/1918
War Diary	Vaux Vraucourt	22/03/1918	24/03/1918
War Diary	Behagnies	24/03/1918	26/03/1918
War Diary	Sus St. Leger.	27/03/1918	28/03/1918
War Diary	Beugin	29/03/1918	01/04/1918
War Diary	School Camp	01/04/1918	03/04/1918
War Diary	I-3-B.8.2	04/04/1918	10/04/1918
War Diary	St. Joseph Institute	11/04/1918	11/04/1918
War Diary	Brandhoek	12/04/1918	13/04/1918
War Diary	Mont Des Cats.	14/04/1918	14/04/1918
War Diary	Locre	15/04/1918	15/04/1918
War Diary	Banada Fernes Camp	16/04/1918	18/04/1918
War Diary	Reninghelst	19/04/1918	20/04/1918
War Diary	Bam Becque	21/04/1918	27/04/1918
War Diary	School Camp	28/04/1918	28/04/1918
War Diary	L.29.6.8.2.	29/04/1918	29/04/1918
War Diary	G 26.C.35.50	30/04/1918	04/05/1918
War Diary	Oloutherfine	05/05/1918	08/05/1918
Heading	177th Trench Mortar Battery August 1918 17th To 31st		
War Diary	Barly	17/08/1918	18/08/1918
War Diary	Gouy Blairville	18/08/1918	18/08/1918
War Diary	Line	19/08/1918	23/08/1918
War Diary	Blairville	23/08/1918	23/08/1918
War Diary	Saulty	23/08/1918	24/08/1918
War Diary	Aire	24/08/1918	24/08/1918
War Diary	Lambres	25/08/1918	26/08/1918
War Diary	St. Venant	26/08/1918	27/08/1918
War Diary	Front Line	28/08/1918	30/08/1918
War Diary	Calonne	31/08/1918	31/08/1918
Heading	177th Trench Mortar Battery September 1918		
War Diary	Calonne	01/09/1918	01/09/1918
War Diary	Lestrem	02/09/1918	02/09/1918
War Diary	Calonne	03/09/1918	03/09/1918
War Diary	Stvenant	03/09/1918	05/09/1918
War Diary	Paradis	06/09/1918	07/09/1918
War Diary	Lestrem	08/09/1918	11/09/1918
War Diary	Corps Main Battle Line	12/09/1918	14/09/1918
War Diary	Line	14/09/1918	30/09/1918
Heading	177th Trench Mortar Battery October 1918		
War Diary	Line	01/10/1918	10/10/1918
War Diary	Fort Rompu	11/10/1918	16/10/1918

War Diary	Bois Grenier	17/10/1918	17/10/1918
War Diary	Mont De Premesques	18/10/1918	18/10/1918
War Diary	Monsen Baroevl	19/10/1918	19/10/1918
War Diary	L'Hempon Pont	20/10/1918	20/10/1918
War Diary	Willems	21/10/1918	22/10/1918
War Diary	Hulans	22/10/1918	22/10/1918
War Diary	Line	22/10/1918	31/10/1918
Heading	177th Trench Mortar Battery November 1918		
War Diary	Line	01/11/1918	15/11/1918
War Diary	Seclin	16/11/1918	30/11/1918
Heading	177th Trench Mortar Battery December 1918		
War Diary	Seclin	01/12/1918	05/12/1918
War Diary	Noeux-Les-Mines	06/12/1918	31/12/1918

WO 95/3623/#9

Brigade Trench Mortar
Battery

59TH DIVISION
177TH INFY BDE

TRENCH MORTAR BTY
APR 1917 – DEC 1918.

59TH DIVISION
177TH INFY BDE

SECRET.

Army Form C. 2118.

WAR DIARY of
LIGHT TRENCH MORTAR BATTERY 177th INFANTRY BRIGADE
INTELLIGENCE SUMMARY
(Erase heading not required.) FOR MONTH OF MARCH 1917

Instructions regarding War Diaries and Intelligence Summaries are contained in F. S. Regs., Part II. and the Staff Manual respectively. Title Pages will be prepared in manuscript.

Place	Date	Hour	Summary of Events and Information	Remarks and references to Appendices
BAYON-VILLERS	MARCH 1		Rest and Training at BAYON-VILLERS	
do	2		do	
do	3		do	
FOUCAUCOURT BELLOY	4		Proceeded by Route March to FOUCAUCOURT	
	5		Route March to the line — Took over positions held by 149th Brigade Light T.M.B — Relief battery in line. 6 guns under T.+C. 22 L ESTREES - VILLERS - CARBONNEL Reconnaissance of front from T.+C. 22 to PC SAUDY BELLOY N.27 a.8.9 ROAD shoot 62 E.S.W FRANCE — Remainder of battery in front line with no employment	
do	6		Trench Mortar Activity nil — Guns left by last battery in front line with no employment or cover for ammunition — new positions reconnoitred	
do	7		Trench Mortar Activity Nil — mud rendered digging of new positions impossible — 1 man went to hospital with rheumatic fever	
do	8		Trench Mortar Activity Nil — new positions reconnoitred 'Ellen' in hand — 33 men & 1 officer H.Q.9 SLEPPED 4/4 LINCOLN REGT Reserve rations attached to bn —	
do	9		Army relieved by Mud half	
do	10		No Mortar Activity — replacement digging continued under very bad conditions	
do	11		No Mortar Activity — replacement digging by night today — a man buried with trench feet	
do	12		2 guns in Right gun'd twenty gun shelter each in salient in German lines — accuracy of fire	
do	13		nil — no retaliation — few details — replacement digging continued	
do	14		Relieved by Mud half — no activity	
do	15		1 gun and 6 men of 178th Bde Light Trench Mortar Battery came up for instruction in trench mortar work Steming no activity	

WAR DIARY

LIGHT TRENCH MORTAR OR BATTERY

INTELLIGENCE SUMMARY 177TH INFANTRY BRIGADE

(Erase heading not required.) for MONTH of MARCH (continued)

Army Form C. 2118.

Place	Date	Hour	Summary of Events and Information	Remarks and references to Appendices
BELLOY	March 16		Battery standing by 11.30 pm ready to put up barrage to assist raid of 2/5 LEICESTER REGT on Right of Front — Raid cancelled at 11.15 p.m. — emplacements completed on left of general line centre	
"	17		3 guns took part in artillery bombardment of German lines from about 120 shells from zero to zero + 5. to assist trench offensive fully SOUTH — Zero 7.30 a.m. — stokes guns fired & then retired from their positions during the night	
"	18		1/2 Battery relieved by M.G. batty. — LIEUT DICKINSON went to hospital with laryngitis	
"	19		1/2 Battery relieved by M.G. in line & concentrated at forward headquarters preparatory to move forward	
"	20		guns collected from positions to Brigade Bomb. officers — Battery relieved by 178th Bgde side by [ill] Stokes collected & handed out & proceeded by Route march to rest billets at FOUCAUCOURT	
	21		Rest at FOUCAUCOURT	
FOUCAUCOURT	22		do. 2/4 LINCOLN REGT	
"	23		do. Lieut. G. SHEPPARD posted to Battery in place of 2/Lieut. G.S. SMITH 2/5 Leicester R95	
"	24		do. & training. — Lieut. G. Sprigdale moved forward to line — Bde. HQ at ETERPIGNY	
"	25		do. & training — Rest of Brigade moved forward to line — Bde HQ ETERPIGNY	
"	26		do. & training. — Reserve battery met reception of NCO & 2 men returned to own unit	
"	27		do.	
"	28		do.	
"	29		Battery proceeded to course of instruction at 4th Army Trench Mortar School at VAUX – ARMENON course of instruction	
	30		do.	
	31		do.	

J.C. Howard Capt.
O.C. Light Trench Mortar Bat.
177 Infantry Bde.

Secret.

Light Trench Mortar Battery
17th Infantry Brigade
April 1st – 30th

Army Form C. 2118.
59

WAR DIARY or INTELLIGENCE SUMMARY
(Erase heading not required.)

Place	Date	Hour	Summary of Events and Information	Remarks and references to Appendices
VAUX-MARMETOS	April 1		In course of Instruction at 5th Army School	
"	2		Do.	
"	3		Do.	
"	4		Do.	
"	5		Do.	
"	6		Do.	
"	7		Do.	
"	8		Do.	
HAMELET	9		Returned to line again - in billets in ruined houses near Bde H.Q's. Map reference K.21.a.0.3 Starts Em.C.	
"	10		Emplacements for guns sited behind line of trenches held by infantry. Both front May Ref L.6.a – L.23.d.	
"	11		Work commenced on two emplacements. Map reference – L.16.a.5.5. – 2 men wounded one Rifleman (being) Battery Sergt-Major	
HESBECOURT	12		Work continued on two emplacements – Battery moved its Headquarters to HESRECOURT L.13.c.1.	
Do.	13		Work continued on emplacements	
Do.	14		Do.	
Do.	15		2 emplacements completed – 2 more started at – L.10.c.5.5	
Do.	16		Work on emplacements continued	
Do.	17		2 emplacements completed 18 April 13.0.R. occupied emplacements in line – no trench mortar activity	
Do.	18		Do.	
FLÉCHIN	19		Brigade went into Bde. Reserve. Orders received by 17th Brigade – Battery went into Rest billets at Fléchin @ 17.a.	
Do.	20		Brigade Rest at Fléchin – Waiting + Cleaning up	
Do.	21		Do.	

J.M.

WAR DIARY or INTELLIGENCE SUMMARY

Army Form C. 2118.

Light Trench Mortar Battery — 177th Infantry Brigade

Place	Date	Hour	Summary of Events and Information	Remarks and references to Appendices
Hébuterne	April 23		Reserve Battery. 2 Officers + 2 O.R. came up for instruction. Training continued.	
do	24		Training continued — Permanent Battery used for wiring Corps line of Defence @ 17a	
do	25		Training continued — do	
do	26		O.C. Battery, Lieut Booco & DICKINSON went up to MONTIGNY FARM SUGAR FACTORY Map Ref K 36 d 0.3 to make arrangements for taking over from 176th Light Trench Mortar Battery who were holding right section of Divisional front. — No emplacements about Reserve day in the line & men of battery were being employed in mending roads — Training of Reserve continued.	
do	27		Relief by Battery of 176th Light T.M. B3 which was then taken place cancelled.	
do	28		Battery relieved 178th Light T.M.B3 at Sugar Factory MONTIGNY FARM. Relief complete 3.p.m.	
do	29		Day Spent in making proper quarters + sanitary arrangements for men	
do	30		Line Reconnoitered for positions — Training of Reserve continued	

J. C. Howard Capt.
O.C. Light Trench Mortar Battery
177th Infantry Bde

To D.A.C.

Back

Herewith War Diary of this Unit for month of May.

J.C. Heward
Capt.
OC
2 M B
177th Inf Bde

[Stamp: LIGHT TRENCH MORTAR BATTERY, No. D372, Date 1-6-17, 177th INFANTRY]

WAR DIARY for MAY 1917
of Flying Trench Mortar Battery, 149th Infantry Brigade
Army Form C. 2118.

INTELLIGENCE SUMMARY
(Erase heading not required.)

Instructions regarding War Diaries and Intelligence Summaries are contained in F.S. Regs., Part II. and the Staff Manual respectively. Title Pages will be prepared in manuscript.

Place	Date	Hour	Summary of Events and Information	Remarks and references to Appendices
SUGAR FACTORY MONTIGNY FARM	MAY 1		Emplacements started on main line of Resistance at L22.c.6.5 (2) L28.d.1.7.3 L23.a.8.6	
do	2		Work continued on Emplacements	
"	3		Do	
"	4		Do	
"	5		Do — Front post of outpost line reconnoitred by O.C. with guns	
"	6		to an attack on BUISSON - GUILAINE FARM. — 2 emplacements started at L34.c.8.7 L34.c.9.4 by night.	
"	7		Work continued on Enforcements	
"	8		2 E.P. Parapets at L22.c.6.5 (2) L28.d.1.7, L28.c.2.6 completed. Harrassment by 16 officers 13.0.R. Work continued by night on two emplacements at L.34.c.8.7 + L34.c.9.4.	
"	9		Work continued on Emplacements	
"	10		Emplacements at L34 c.8.7 + L34.c.9.4 completed	
"	11		Relief of Garrison officer on line relieved — officer in line relieved carried out.	
"	12		Officer in line relieved — Vacancies of battery other than Line bathed at Bath at SUGAR FACTORY.	
"	13		Portion of men used to make Battalion Headquarters at R.S.a	
"	14		Gunners taken out of the line preparatory to relief Division going into rest + relief taken over by Cavalry Division without Trench Mortars —	
VRAIGNES	15		Battery proceeded by route march into Rest Billets at VRAIGNES. Major R.J. Dyne a.g-8	
do	16		Battery engaged in cleaning up.	
do	17		Cleaning of Battery and Review started	
do	18		Drawing ditto	

Army Form C. 2118.

WAR DIARY or INTELLIGENCE SUMMARY of Light Trench Mortar Battery 174th Infantry Bde.

(Erase heading not required.)

Instructions regarding War Diaries and Intelligence Summaries are contained in F.S. Regs., Part II. and the Staff Manual respectively. Title Pages will be prepared in manuscript.

Place	Date	Hour	Summary of Events and Information	Remarks and references to Appendices
VIDAIGNES	MAY 19		Training continued – football in the afternoon	
do	20		duto.	
do	21		O.C. Battery went to the H.Qrs. 174th Infantry Bde. ROISEL preparatory to relieving the 173rd T.M.B. Training continues.	
do.	22		O.C. Battery + 2 Officers + 21 O.R. paraded by Route March to link and relieved 176th T.M.B. in 2 Emplacements at L6.c.0.3 and 2 Emplacements at L10 cm central. Remainder of Personnel + Remer Batteries continued training at Vidaignes in morning – Sports in afternoon.	
do	23		Emplaced at L6.c.0.3 fired about 40 rounds at suspected Trench Mortar + machine Gun Emplacements at L5.b.8.4. and a point from which Machine Gun fire was opening. Nightly at L12.a.3.6. 6 round belts fired on the Battalion Trench at F30.c. and L6.a. Personnel + Marine Battery sentenced receiving Gas targets fired on Experience days.	
do	24		Trench Mortar enquired at L12.a.9.B fired on enemy	
L10.a.Central	25		Permanent Battery jouraded by Rifle Grenade Sounds L.G.A. disposal by a Germans Stonewall of (Battery employed in making Billets at Headquarters and Section Troops in Trench Mortar work 2 N.C.O.'s instructing with Cavalry composed of men behaving Dragoons and Indian troops. Patrol NCO proceeded to line. Germans hammering effort firing in Sassing in L.5.d. after approach was fired from Stokes Mortar.	
L10.a.Central	26		Training of L.G. Courage outbreaks employment. 1 NCO returns from his two furlough. Remainder of Battery continues working on Billets or Headquarters.	
L.10.a.Central	27		Retaliation fire opened by 2 mortars in L.S.d. after German Minenwerfer had opened fire. Range aug 570 yds. Fire of Minenwerfer opposed position approx approximately was located at G.1.c.7.4.	

WAR DIARY
INTELLIGENCE SUMMARY

Army Form C. 2118.

G. Lykes James Marton Battery
177th Infantry Brigade

(Erase heading not required.)

Place	Date	Hour	Summary of Events and Information	Remarks and references to Appendices
L.10.a.Central	May 28	6.30pm	Attempts to establish a post made by troops holding Nelnut, on the junction of the NEW and ENFILADE trench at L.6.a.4.6. under the portion of the NEW trench S. of the junction. A barrage was put up by 2.5'' Stokes Mortars in there 2 trenches. The barrage was timed by one gun on ENFILADE trench at L.6.a.6.7, and on the NEW trench at L.6.a.4.5. Rapid fire was opened for first 3 minutes. After the starting party had left the trenches followed by an intense bombardment of 10 rounds per minute. The barrage was maintained at this on the ENFILADE trench and after being 150 yrds at first settled down on the NEW trench on the working party going rather far up the NEW trench the barrage was shifted further South. The working party were unsuccessful in bringing back documents or badges to identify the Regiments opposite us.	
		12.30pm	Stokes fire on the Quarry, L.S.Q, fired 30 rounds in 40. Enemy went in Railway Cutting at L.12.a.4.7. – Silence of Enemy Batteries.	
L.10.a.Central	29	2pm	About 20 rounds fired at 2 or 3 of Enemy firemen New Trench at L.6.a. Enemy were seen to run amongst ENFILADE Trench. Discovery of one Indian officer, 2 N.C.O's and 9 men of CENTRAL INDIAN HORSE and one Officer, 1 Sergeant, 4 Corporals and 9 men of INNISKILLING DRAGOONS COMPLETED. 1.8m fuse Repetition shots at recovering with Manvneures of H.2. Enemy retaliated energetically with Maroncamps Thraws about 30 rounds of 4.2 Howitzers. No Casualties or materiel.	
L.10.a Central	30		2 guns fired on junction of NEW & ENFILADE trenches & also on a sniping post in these trenches. 4 rounds were all fired at L.6.7.5 (Cross Road Farm)	
do	31			

J.C. Howard Capt.
Officer Light Trench Mortar Batty
177th Infantry Bgde

SECRET

Army Form C. 2118.

Map ref. Sheet 62 C N.E. + 62 B N.W
Edition 3A 57 C S.E

JUNE 1917

By the Light Trench Mortar Battery
177th Infantry Brigade

WAR DIARY
or
INTELLIGENCE SUMMARY.
(Erase heading not required.)

Instructions regarding War Diaries and Intelligence Summaries are contained in F. S. Regs., Part II. and the Staff Manual respectively. Title pages will be prepared in manuscript.

Hour, Date, Place	Summary of Events and Information	Remarks and References to Appendices
6 a.m. JUNE 1 L.10.c.4.5.	11 Rounds were fired by 2 Stokes Mortars in Retaliation for Light Minenwerfer firing on our trenches from near SUGAR FACTORY in G.1.b.15. Minenwerfer ceased firing. New emplacements started in quarry L.5.d.	JWH
4.45 p.m. 2 Do.	Gun fires in suspected M.G. emplacement in trench L.6.C.25. Two direct hits obtained.	JWH
7.30 p.m. 2 Do.	3 Shots fired at men seen working at new M.G. emplacement at L.6.a.4.6. First shot on parapet while second fell in the trench. Work continued in new emplacement.	JWH
6.0 a.m. 3 Do.	Retaliation fire opened on Farm 200 yds NE. (unnamed) FARM L.6.a.12.0. for several Minenwerfer shots which had fallen on our trench. Afterwards the German mortar ceased firing. Work continued on new emplacement in quarry.	JWH
Do. 4	2 Shots fired at suspected new M.G. emplacement in trench L.6.C.2.5. Both shots landed in trench. Minenwerfer more feared at suspected emplacement. Minenwerfer in retaliation for 2 rounds fired by enemy	JWH

Maps. Rfs. France Sheet 62 °NE - 62 °NW.
Edition 7A.

JUNE 1917
Army Form C. 2118.

Maps of the Light Trench Mortar Battery
177th Infantry Brigade

WAR DIARY
INTELLIGENCE SUMMARY.
(Erase heading not required.)

Hour, Date, Place	Summary of Events and Information	Remarks and References to Appendices
JUNE 4 L.10.c.5. (cont.)	Work continued on new position in Quarry. Relief of 1 Officer & 16 O.R. by another Officer & 16 O.R. carried out at 10.30 p.m.	J.W.
5 Do.	Very little trench mortar activity. The Cooley Line received fire of 4 bursting retaliation on the part of the enemy. Pattern of Battery taken.	J.W.
6 Do.	3 rounds fired on enemy's Trench M.G. Post in neighbourhood at SOUTH of CROSS ROADS FARM L.6.a.9.1. 5 rounds in Enfy. of enemy in NEW TRENCH L.6.a. Work continued on new emplacements to Quarry L.5.d.	J.W.
3.30 a.m. 7 Do.	Several rounds fired on enemy working parties & ammunition of NEW - ENFILADE Trench L.6.a.	J.W.
5.0 a.m.	15 rounds fired in retaliation for Minenwerfer fire in vicinity L.5.d.
5.0 a.m.	Colonel PEGNEY, N.C.O in charge of LEFT SECTOR, carried recce as to Aft. place where hostile Battery & Enemy marked of fired. Report + supplements with M.S.S. Burst in Aft. land gun. T.M.L.S.E. inflicted slight damage to gun between now in pit to to the same. Dep. on Distaster Quarry receives reference 1st.
8 Do.	Little trench mortar activity. Work continued on dug-out in Quarry. W. DAVIS parts of rifle & cradle handed over to Mentor. Relief of 1 Officer 16 O.R. carried out at 10.p.m (usual) arrived in L.O.R. M.N. LSe.y in afternoon with 4.25 x 5.9 5

JUNE 1917

Army Form C. 2118.

Trench Map Ref. France Sheet 62 ONE, 62 ONW
Edition 3A

The Right Grenadier Battery
17th Infantry Brigade

WAR DIARY
or
INTELLIGENCE SUMMARY.
(Erase heading not required.)

Hour, Date, Place	Summary of Events and Information	Remarks and References to Appendices
11 p.m.	9. L.10.a.4.5. Little activity until front line. Work continues on dugout in gunpit.	
	10. Do. 2 front mortars in gunpit. Had a position fired in COLOGNE FARM L6a.2.8. 7.m during the day and patrol relieved the COLOGNE FARM sequence. No reaction. Enemy fired a patrol, did not succeed in reaching COLOGNE FARM. Another trench mortar fired in position of NEW COMMS trench, L6a, to avoid patrol. No casualties. Dugout in gunpit continues.	
9.40 p.m	11. Do. Two new pits into NEW LINE returned to CROSS ROADS FARM L6.9.1 at [unclear] Manoeuvre employment. His reaction after that from his position with a dugout continues.	
12.30 a.m.	12. Do. Enemy mortars active for 1 hour. Lt. SHEPPARD's dugout was hit and demolished first shot. Lt. SHEPPARD got wall-shock and is being treated.	
11 p.m.	Work on the dugout in NEW LINE and NEW trench a bombproof [unclear] by 1 John [unclear] 6 minutes the dugout now [unclear] to fix [unclear] 2 pits per [unclear] during the [unclear] the enemy [unclear] one lewis gun pit 10 yds up EGYPT [unclear] the road [unclear] [unclear] of NEW trench. Right 10 [unclear] the enemy [unclear] about 80 rounds all together Work in gunpit continued, also mounting of have (?) [unclear] A Stokes was called at L6d.0.3. Continued.	
	13. Do. Very little trench activity. Work on new dugout in road.	
3.45 a.m.	14. Do. Enemy attacked from [unclear] [unclear] in UNNAMED FARM L6a.2a in [unclear] Fire started at 100 string from direction of COLOGNE FARM L6c	

WAR DIARY
INTELLIGENCE SUMMARY

Army Form C. 2118.

Trench Map Ref 62 °NE + 62 °NW.
Edition 3A

JUNE 1917

7th Light Trench Mortar Battery
177th Infantry Brigade

Hour, Date, Place	Summary of Events and Information	Remarks and References to Appendices
3.45 a.m. 14 L10a+b	Taken from E.H.T. Our Mortars was immediately brought into action on enemy who had effected entry from L6e 2.7. Another fired from L5d 4.08 into road junction. One of our observers saw the Bosche bringing up reinforcements & both guns attacks were driven off. Also had mortar ranged & put into position during the day so as to keep off any further attack on UNNAMED FARM. Work in day got continued.	
15 Do	Very little trench mortar activity. Work on dugs continued.	
16 Do	Battery relieved by 176 L.T.M.B. at 7.30 p.m. Battery was billeted at NOISEL for night.	
17 8.30 a.m. Do	Battery proceeded to join 177th Inf. Bde, proceeding by route march to COURCELCOURT WOOD Q.34a.	
18.	Battery under canvas in wood. Battery resting. Men bathed.	
19 Do	Do	
20 Do	Reconnaissance for Mortar position	

WAR DIARY

INTELLIGENCE SUMMARY.

JUNE 1917   Army Form C. 2118.

of the Light Trench Mortar Battery
177th Infantry Brigade

(Erase heading not required.)

Hour, Date, Place	Summary of Events and Information	Remarks and references to Appendices
21 - Q.28.c.2.4.	Battery resting.	J.W.
22. V.10.b.5.3	Battery moved into Brigade Rest Camp at EQUANCOURT	J.W.
23.	Battery resting - Football.	J.W.
24.	— Church parade.	
25.	Training of Battery in morning - men inoculated in afternoon	J.W.
26.	Orders received for two guns to be got into position in Regtl Buzoes (BEAUCHAMP) sector. O.C Battery & Lt. T.P. Dickman rode to 179th Brigade H.Qrs., also Major Kilgour Reserve Trenches Q.6.d.3.8 & made arrangements for two guns being placed in position in this Run testing offrs Inoculation.	J.W.
27.	Men resting after inoculation. Lt. T.P. Dickman & 2 N.C.O's proceeded to Q.18.b.6.6 with two guns Teams for am. ought supplied by 2/6th Sherwood Foresters. Am. expended; bomb at ? 7.4.3: an Explosive bomb at [illegible]	J.W.

WAR DIARY
or INTELLIGENCE SUMMARY.

of the Light Trench Mortar Battery
177th Infantry Brigade

JUNE 1917 Army Form C. 2118.

(Erase heading not required.)

Hour, Date, Place	Summary of Events and Information	Remarks and references to Appendices
JUNE EQUANCOURT		
28 Y.10.b.5.3	Battery training. Sports in afternoon. 6-0.P.M. 2 teams selected from 1/5th Sherwood Foresters on guns in the line. Gun explained at 4 P.M. to 4.30 P.M.	yes
29 Do.	Battery training. Sports in afternoon.	yes
30 Do.	Battery dinner. Battery - Lt. Battery & Lieut. J.S. Davis proceeding to line preparatory to Brigade relieving the 176th Inf. Bde.	yes

J.C. Howard Capt.
O.C.
177th L.T.M.B.

Map Ref: Issues sheet 57c S.E. Position 3A
57c S.W. " 3A

SECRET

Army Form C. 2118.

WAR DIARY
of the 144th Light Trench Mortar Battery
144th Infantry Brigade
INTELLIGENCE SUMMARY
(Erase heading not required.)

JULY 1917

Instructions regarding War Diaries and Intelligence Summaries are contained in F.S. Regs., Part II. and the Staff Manual respectively. Title pages will be prepared in manuscript.

Place	Date	Hour	Summary of Events and Information	Remarks and References to Appendices
V.10.b.5.3	July 1		Church Parade - Zuich. 10th M. Xxxx. and 10 men proceeded to BEAUCAMP SECTOR and relieved Zuick. F.P. Dickinson men in the line.	
Q.20.a.1.1	2		Remainder of Battery proceeded by Route March to METZ, where the Battery installed in dugouts, map ref. Q.20.a.1.1.	
do	3		Battery all went on improving billets. Division transferred from IV to III Army.	
do	4		Battery training.	
do	5		do. Working party at night digging emplacements in Bellon Sector. Major J. 2 Emplacements at Q.5.C.7.9 & 2 at Q.5.a.3.3.	
do	6		Battery Training - Remain proceeded to BARASTRE to help in construction of new camp - nightly working parties on emplacements - Lieut Henry & a party returned from duty with 178th Brigade. Pte. Wittmann wounded during relief - Zuick. Xxxx parties proceeded to Equancourt camp for the night.	
do	7		Battery Training - Zuick Xxxx men marched at Hd Qs Q.16 (Q.20.a.1.1) Working Party on emplacements at night.	
do	8		Battery Training - Working party on Emplacements at night. 2 Emplacements at Q.5.c.7.9 & 2 at Q.5.d.33. completed.	
do	9		do.	
Q.16.Central	10	9.0 am	Battery proceeded by Route March to new camp BARASTRE - Division relieved by 58th Division - Division transferred from III to Corps to IV Corps.	
do	11		Battery Training - Football etc afternoon.	

SECRET

Army Form C. 2118.

Maps referred FRANCE sheet 57c SE Edition 3A
57c SH " 5A

WAR DIARY
or
INTELLIGENCE SUMMARY
(Erase heading not required.)

of 177th Light Trench Mortar Battery
177th Infantry Brigade

JULY 1917.

Instructions regarding War Diaries and Intelligence Summaries are contained in F. S. Regs., Part II. and the Staff Manual respectively. Title pages will be prepared in manuscript.

PLACE	DATE	HOUR	Summary of Events and Information	Remarks and References to Appendices
O.16.central	July 12		Battery training — afternoon frothier etc.	
do	13		do — do — Battery Commander returned from leave.	
do	14		do — do — cricket	
do	15		School Parade.	
do	16		Battery training — afternoon football matches	
do	17		do " do	
do	18		do " do	
do	19		do " do — Divisions at Jumping & Transport competition	
do	20		do " do — Divisional Polo in afternoon	
do	21		do " do.	
do	22		Kn 98 Officers buried to do. IV Corps Scho. 130 V 55	
do	23		Church Parade. No.1 Chair clip of Trench Launch Brigade Tactical Scheme successfully conducted in shooting attack. Experiment — no more RAPD " in Stokes shells	See operation order attached Appendix 1
do	24		message across. Battery Training — O.C. Battery reconnoitred ground for Divisional Circuit & Teuva attack at V.1.8.-70.20.	
do	25"		Battery training and experiment evaluation with Ballistite Caps	

Army Form C. 2118.

WAR DIARY
of 4.9.45 TRENCH MORTAR BATTERY
177th Inf. Bde.

INTELLIGENCE SUMMARY.
(Erase heading not required.)

Place	Date	Hour	Summary of Events and Information	Remarks and References to Appendices
DIB CENTRAL	JULY 26		Mortar Training - lectures etc in afternoon	J.C.H
do	27		Divisional Defence Scheme No:1. Anticipating of Enemy to Zinnel Attack.	J.C.H See Revised instructions appendix II
do	28		Practical Exercise of previous experience by 177th S. Bde.	J.C.H
do	29		Schools Parades	J.C.H
do	30		Battery training — schools afternoon	J.C.H
do	31		Battery parades	J.C.H

J.C. Howard Capt.
OC. 177 Light Trench Mortar Battery

APPENDIX II

SECRET. 177th Inf. Bde. Copy No. 6
Tactical Scheme No. 1.
Operation Order No. 1.

22.7.17.

Reference Map Sheet 57C S.W. & 1/10,000 Trench Map Ypres

1. On 25th July the 177th Inf. Bde Brigade will attack the enemy & finalise objectives O.21.c.7.0.9.5 & O.22.a.0.11.4. At the same time X Brigade will attack with four and Y Bde. on the right.

2. [illegible handwritten paragraph]

3. [illegible handwritten paragraph]

4. [illegible handwritten paragraph]

the Barrage at Zero plus 04, and will remain
under orders of the O.C. 7th London Regt.

5.   No. 3 & 4 Guns of this Bty. will be attached to
1/8th London Regt. and will advance with the second
line of the Bn & come into action some 100 does
in the first German position about the point
O.22.a.2.4. These two guns will be under the
command of   Capt.   Hamerdyer and will reinforce
Guns of 1/8th London Regt.

6.   No. 5 & 6 Guns of this Bty. will commence
rate of fire per min accord.   Must have had nearer
with Lewis Road. & Rgmt. messages from
Battalns. & Companies of the assaulting
Battalion to Brigade Headquarters who will
have made a Receiving Station at O.22.a.?.f.
To take position Bn   in case w/ned of the
taking part in the Barrage.

7.   No. 7 & 8 guns of the Indep. will take position at
Right Communication Trench & H.Q. & are to be
at O.21.d. J.10. some will be held in reserve.
These two guns will advance on receiving
word to do so from the Battery Commander when the
second objective has been taken.

8.   Carrying parties of 4 men each and
detachment accompanied by The Lewis & 1/15
London Regts. They will be attached to

each detachments and go forward with their detachments. They will take forward stores showing the notices of the dumps formed in the enemy front line. They will dump their stores in excavations in the Road opposite the position to which the guns have been moved.

9. Detachment Commanders will synchronize watches at 9.30 a.m. on the 23rd inst. on the Battery Parade Ground

10. Battery H.Qrs. will be at H.Qrs. 1/5 Lincoln Regt. in Right Communication Trench. Advanced H.Qrs. will be in Sunken Road at O.22.a.2.6.

11. Position of H.Qrs. Dumps R.A.P's & predoms C.Ts. as shown in attached map.

12. Dumps for rations, water & Stokes Shell will be
   Right Battalion   O.16.c.1.2
   Left   do   O.22.a.2.8

13. Barrage time table as shown on attached map.

14. Zero hour will be 11 A.M.

15. Troops will be in position at zero minus half an hour.

Issued to:
Copy No 1. 177th Inf. Bde.
  "   " 2. 1/4 Lincoln Regt.
  "   " 3. 1/5 Lincoln Regt.
  "   " 4. 177th M.G. Coy.
  "   " 5. War Diary
  "   " 6. War Diary.

J. C. Howard
Capt.
O.C.
L.T.M.B.
177th Inf. Bde.

SECRET   APPENDIX II   COPY. No:- 7
59th DIVISIONAL TACTICAL EXERCISE No:- 1.
177th Light Trench Mortar Battery Operation
                    Order. No:- 6.
Reference   Sheet 57c S.W. Maps A.B.C. attached 25/7/17

1. On July 27th the 59th Division will attack the
enemy's trenches between N.6.b.90.20 & N.36.d.40.20
       At the same time the "M" Division will
attack on the Right & the "N" Division on the left
of the 59th Division.

2.   The attack of the 59th Division will be
made by the 178th Brigade on the Right and
the 177th Brigade on the left. The objectives
of the Brigades are:-
       (a) The German ~~trench~~ front line trench.
       (b) STAR trench & MOON trench.
       (c) TREACLE Trench.
              Each objective when captured will
be consolidated. The dividing line between
the 177th & 178th Brigades is shown on the
attached sketch map "A".

3.   After the capture of Treacle Trench the
176th Infantry Brigade will pass through
the 177th & 178th Bdes. and will consolidate
a ~~front~~ position in continuation of
PROMETHEUS TRENCH. through O.32.central
and WINDMILL MOUND to the main PERONNE
- BAPAUME ~~road~~.

Simultaneously with the attack of the 176th Bde. the 200th Bde of the "N"th Division is to attack PROMETHEUS TRENCH and the 210th Bde of the Nth Division is to gain the eastern edge of LE TRANSLOY.

The Artillery Barrage is shown on the attached map sketch "B".

5. The attack of the 177th I.J. Bde. will be made by the 2/4 LINCOLNS on the right and the 2/5 LINCOLNS on the left.

Dividing line as shown on MAP "A"

Each objective when captured will be consolidated.

The leap frog system of attack will be adopted.

6. The 177th Light Trench Mortar Battery will be in position in our front line trench and will assist artillery barrage firing as under:—

No: 1 Gun — junction of C.T. & enemy front line at U.4.a.8.8.

No: 2 Gun — junction of C.T. & enemy front line at O.31.c.05.05.

No: 3 Gun — junction of C.T. & enemy front line at N.36.d.9.1.

No: 4 Gun — Trench junction N.36.d.5.1.

" 5+6 " " " N.36.d.85.25

" 7 Gun " " MARS C.T. & MEAN trench O.31.c.1.4.

No. 8 Gun — junction of AVENUE C.T. & MEAN trench O.31.c.35.35.

These guns will cease fire with
Artillery Barrage as follows:—
Nos. 1, 2, 5 & 6 will fire from +3 to +11.
Nos. 3 & 4   will fire from zero to +8.
Nos. 7 & 8   will fire from +7 to +15.
The rate of fire will be 10 rounds per minute.

Nos. 3 & 4 Guns after taking part in the Barrage will come under the command of the O.C. 1/4 LINCOLN REGT. and will move forward in accordance with orders received from him.

Nos. 5 & 6 Guns after taking part in the Barrage will come under the orders of the O.C. 1/5 Lincoln Regt. and will advance in accordance with orders received from him.

Nos. 1, 2, 7 & 8 Guns on the capture of the third objective will move forward to MOON TRENCH and will rendezvous as follows:—
No. 1 & 2 at junction of AVENUE and MOON Trench & No. 7 & 8 at junction of MARS & MOON trench. These Guns will take up positions and make emplacements so that a barrage can be put down in front of our TRENCH trench in case of enemy counter attack.

an enemy counter attack.

7. Flares will be lit by the advance line at Zero + 30 minutes.

8. Positions of Headquarters, dumps, R.A.P.'s as shown on the map. Battery Hd. Qrs. will be established at T.6.b.3.8.

9. Carrying parties will be supplied at the rate of 2 men + 1 N.C.O. per detachment by either 2/4 Lincolns or P/5 Lincoln Regt.

10. Zero hour will be 9·0 A.M.

11. Lieut Steven will attend at Bde. H.Qrs. at 5·40 A.M. 27th inst. for the synchronisation of watches.

J.C. Howard

Copy No. 1 177th Inf Bde
    2 2/4 Lincoln Regt.   Capt.
    3 P/5 Lincoln Regt.   O.C.
  4+5 Motor Ramparts   T.M.B.
    6 War Diary   177th Inf Bde
    7 War Diary

SECRET

Army Form C. 2118.

Map Reference Trones 57c SE Edition 3a.
57c SW " 5a.

WAR DIARY
of Light Trench Mortar Battery 174th Infantry Bde.
INTELLIGENCE SUMMARY.
(Erase heading not required.)

August 1917.

Instructions regarding War Diaries and Intelligence Summaries are contained in F. S. Regs., Part II. and the Staff Manual respectively. Title pages will be prepared in manuscript.

Place	Date	Hour	Summary of Events and Information	Remarks and references to Appendices
O. 16- central	1		Battery Training — Afternoon football - Cricket.	JM
	2		" Bathing — ditto	JM
	3		" Training — ditto	JM
	4		" ditto — ditto — afternoon Divisional Horseus No. 2 fun Officers	JM
	5		" ditto — ditto	JM
	6		Church Parade.	JM
	7		Battery Training. Afternoon football.	JM
	8		do do	JM
	9		do do	JM
	10		do do Lt. Flenn proceeded on leave.	JM
	11		do do	JM
	12		Divisional Toureus No. 3. consisting of Lunch to Lunch attack	JM
	13		Church Parade.	JM
	14		Battery Training. Bathing — Afternoon football etc.	JM
	15		Brigade Trench to Lunch attack afternoon football etc.	JM
	16		Battery Training — football	JM
	17		do. do	JM
	18		do. do.	JM
	19		Church Parade.	JM
	20		Battery Junior Musketry Course.	JM

SECRET
Army Form C. 2118.

WAR DIARY
144th Light Inf.
INTELLIGENCE SUMMARY.
(Erase heading not required.)

Instructions regarding War Diaries and Intelligence Summaries are contained in F. S. Regs., Part II. and the Staff Manual respectively. Title pages will be prepared in manuscript.

Place	Date	Hour	Summary of Events and Information	Remarks and references to Appendices
O.16.Central	21		Battery Training – afternoon football cricket etc.	
do.	22	7.0pm	Battery Paraded in lorries & moved to Tincourt (SE.N.v.18)	
SENLIS (P.b.d.s.v)	23		Battery Training – Cricket Football etc.	
do.	24		do.	
do.	25		do.	
do.	26		Church Parade	
do.	27		Battery Training	
do.	28		do.	
do.	29		do. Preparing to move.	
do.	30		do. & entrained at ROUEN	
WINNEZEELE (J.10.a.8.6)	31	11.0pm	Battery detrained at ROUEN & proceeded by foot march Winnezeele area.	

D. Kent
Lieut.
144th L.T.M.B.

Map reference Belgium & France Sheet 2y Edition 2

Army Form C. 2118.

WAR DIARY
or of the 197th Light Trench Mortar Battery
INTELLIGENCE SUMMARY. for September 1917.
(Erase heading not required.)

Instructions regarding War Diaries and Intelligence Summaries are contained in F. S. Regs., Part II. and the Staff Manual respectively. Title pages will be prepared in manuscript.

Place	Date	Hour	Summary of Events and Information	Remarks and references to Appendices
WINNE ZEELE	1		Battery training etc — Football etc in afternoon	
	2		Church Parade	
	3		Battery Training — Football etc in afternoon	
	4		ditto — ditto	
	5		ditto — ditto	
	6		ditto — ditto	
			Lieut. J. Shaw proceeds on leave. Lewis Gunners	
	7		2nd. Lieut. went to POPERINGHE to Corps School. to see the arrival of the Japan Guest	
	8		Battery Training — Football in afternoon	
	9		Church Parade	
	10		Battery Training — Football etc	
	11		do do	
	12		do do	
	13		do do	
	14		do do	
	15		Salvage Parade (Brigade operation)	
	16		Battery Training — Football etc	
	17		do do	
	18		do do	
	19		do do	
LUNA PARK	20		Battery proceeded by route march to LUNA PARK.	
	21		Training	
	22		ditto	

WAR DIARY or INTELLIGENCE SUMMARY

Army Form C. 2118.

SEPTEMBER 1917

Place	Date	Hour	Summary of Events and Information	Remarks and references to Appendices
Goldfish Chateau	23		Battery proceeded by own route march to Goldfish Chateau.	
WIELTJE	24		Battery proceeded to Trenches at WIELTJE.	
	25	10:00 am	Bt Battery moved to & visited line and formed up position prior to the attack.	
		8:00 pm	Bt Battery moved to Kerne r Blt Lithelant proceeded to the line and chose forward position off by digging implements at D.20.a.25.35 and D.20.a.55.0 and 35.35. The Guns on the line were put in emergency strong points and held there at D.20.a.75.80, D.14.o.60.25, D.20.a.75. Just prior to the infantry attacking the action had the effect of silencing two enemy machine guns at two points not in attacking zone not a key point owing to the teams. Guns which were subsequently captured with the teams. After the guns teams stood by ready to go if an event arose, the party of No were held up by any machine gun points or machine guns known not called upon. Soon after the infantry had advanced then guns appeared. They made there my lightly sketchy headquarters. Now if the gun crew was kept out of action during the attack but not before they completed the task. Thereminder of battery was under forward for carrying parties for ammunition the son her no major actions for the moment. The casualties were not heavy. Lt.Col. & Lt. Urchion left the line for infantry during intervention. The James Infantry slightly (GSW) Battery returned to Brandon to entrain. Carrying parties for ammunition.	
	26			
	27			
	28			
	29			
	30			

Makefuure HAZEBROUCK,5.A.ED.2.
FRANCE 36c 9N. Ed. 10A.

ORIGINAL. SECRET.

WAR DIARY of the 197¹ Light Trench Mortar Battery

INTELLIGENCE SUMMARY.
(Erase heading not required.)

OCTOBER 1917

Army Form C. 2118.

Instructions regarding War Diaries and Intelligence Summaries are contained in F. S. Regs., Part II. and the Staff Manual respectively. Title pages will be prepared in manuscript.

Place	Date	Hour	Summary of Events and Information	Remarks and references to Appendices
Vlamertinghe (Brandy)	1		Battery cleaning up etc.	
2½-2-3	2		" Preparing to move to new area	
		Noon	" " Entrained at VLAMERTINGHE and detrained at THIENNES. Thence by motor lorries to	
HAMET BILLET (Makefuure 5.6.2.4.).				
HAMET BILLET	3		Batterys cleaning up arms, inspecting billets etc.	
do	4		" training - afternoon football etc.	
do	5		do as	
ERNY ST. JULIEN	6		Battery proceeded by motor such lorries to ERNY ST. JULIEN	
do	7		Church Parade.	
do	8		Battery training - afternoon football etc.	
do	9		do as	
BOURS	10		Battery proceeded by route march to FERFAYS AREA & were billeted for one night at BOURS.	
MAISNIL LE RUITZ	11		" " " " BRUAY AREA & " " " " MAISNIL-LE-RUITZ	
			Lieut. J.P. Brockman went on leave. Lieut. Bauer proceeded to the line preparatory to taking over from the 3rd CANADIAN T.M.B.	
VANCOUVER CAMP	12		Battery proceeded by route march to VANCOUVER CAMP and were billeted for one night.	
AVION	13		6 am Guns took over emplacements and guns in the HIGH SECTOR. Headquarters were established at S.18.A.3.5. - Emplacements of guns (1) T.3.9. (2) T.3.a.30.90. (3) M.32.d.60.65. (4) M.32.b.55.25. (5) M.32.b.57.30. (6) M.32.b.57.35.- Captain Gildersleeve returned	
	14		to Units from Hospital. No trench mortar activity	

A5834 Wt. W4973/M687 750,000 8/16 D. D. & L. Ltd. Form/C.2118/13.

SECRET.

Intelligence Summary of the 141st Light Trench Mortar Battery
Source Sheet 36.S.W.3a.10a.
Trench Map 36c.S.E.Ed.9.   Army Form C. 2118.

WAR DIARY

INTELLIGENCE SUMMARY of the 141st Light Trench Mortar Battery.

October 1917 (Continued)

(Erase heading not required.)

Instructions regarding War Diaries and Intelligence
Summaries are contained in F.S. Regs., Part II.
and the Staff Manual respectively. Title pages
will be prepared in manuscript.

Place	Date	Hour	Summary of Events and Information	Remarks and references to Appendices
AVION	15		No Trench Mortar Activity	JCH
	16		New Emplacements dug at T.3.a.80.80, T.3.a.75.75. for No 1 & 2 Guns. Gun Emplacement.	JCH
N.31.c.9.1.	17		Headquarters moved to T.4.COULOTTE. H.Q's formed at H.Q's of Left Battalion (N.31.c.9.1).	JCH
	18		No T.M. activity	JCH
	19		Several rounds fired at Enemy Trench mortar positions in Railway Embankment at N.33.d. Jim Offensive positions at T.3.a.9.9.	JCH
	20		About 30 shots fired at night on enemy targets.	JCH
	21		Battery Moved by 141 L.T.M.B. went by rail to rest billets at Gouy Servins. Jim " " H.Q's at Q.35.d.0.8.	JCH
Gouy Servins Q.33.d.0.6.	22		Battery cleaning up.	JCH
	23		" Drawing	JCH
	24		" "	JCH
	25		" Drawing & Bathing	JCH
	26		" Afternoon Football	JCH
	27		" H.Artayne & Mt.Saso (1st Leicesters) attacked to instruction (Dismounted)	JCH
	28		O.C. Battery & 2IC in command went to the line to arrange for relief from the 176 L.T.M.B.	JCH
	29		Battery training – Lectures returned to the Battalion (1st Leicesters)	JCH
	30		Battery released the 176 L.T.M.B. taking 5 guns into positions in the line, kept reinforcements from 0.16.19.75.35. 9/15	JCH
N.23.d.1.9.	31	(2) N.19.b.25.40.(3) N.19.6.90.20.(4) N.15.c.9.28.(5) N.18.c.90.20. and one gun in reserve at M.23.d.1.9. About 60 rounds fired through the day night at Positions M.G. Emplacements, Sick Gun & Dugouts. No activity during the day and night. Sketch given also Lewis Post on discharge of gas dischargers	JCH
				JCH

J.C. Henwort
Capt
O.C. 141 L.T.M.B.

SECRET

Army Form C. 2118.

MAP REFERENCES
SHEET 36 S.W.1. (Edition 9A)

ORIGINAL

WAR DIARY
of the 177th LIGHT TRENCH MORTAR BATTERY
INTELLIGENCE SUMMARY.
NOVEMBER 1917

(Erase heading not required.)

Instructions regarding War Diaries and Intelligence Summaries are contained in F. S. Regs., Part II. and the Staff Manual respectively. Title pages will be prepared in manuscript.

Place	Date	Hour	Summary of Events and Information	Remarks and references to Appendices
M23.b.6.2.	1		About 40 Rounds fired during the night onto day at enemy machine gun position, trench Mortar Emplacements and company Shelters in N.14.c, N.20.a. + N.20.c	*(appx)*
	2		About 60 Rounds fired during the night at various selected targets in same areas	*(appx)*
	3		70 Rounds fired on selected Targets in same areas	*(appx)*
	4		do. do.	*(appx)*
	5		70 do. do.	*(appx)*
			Harassing fire during night and day. At night Barrage kept up on selected targets during night + day. Relief of left section by right section at middle of 16 days tour carried out.	*(appx)*
	6		1 a.m. to noon listening patrols of 7th R. Irish Regt. who were acting in formation and endeavours to secure prisoners Regt. were during the operation. Altogether during the day 130 rounds were fired.	*(appx)*
	7		59 Rounds fired during the operation at N.20.a.	*(appx)*
			90 Rounds harrassing fire during the day on M.G. Emplacements, 2 M position and Coy. Hd. Qrs. etc. in N.14.c + N.20.a.	*(appx)*
	8		80 Rounds fired at selected Targets in open area.	*(appx)*
	9		80 Rounds fired at selected Targets – trench bosses and trenches which grew in left section emplaced began to fall in.	*(appx)*
	10		About 80 Rounds during the course of the day at selected targets – An Artillery Bombardment was carried out in the morning and 90 rounds were fired from 2 guns on left during the course of this – Drums on left answer	*(appx)*
M23.b.6.5.	11		About 90 Rounds were fired during the day at various targets	*(appx)*

SECRET

Army Form C. 2118.

MAP REFERENCE FRANCE 36c SW
FRANCE 51c
FRANCE 57c

WAR DIARY
of 177th Light Trench Mortar Battery 177th INF. BDE.

INTELLIGENCE SUMMARY
(Erase heading not required.)

NOVEMBER - 1917

Instructions regarding War Diaries and Intelligence Summaries are contained in F.S. Regs., Part II. and the Staff Manual respectively. Title pages will be prepared in manuscript.

Place	Date	Hour	Summary of Events and Information	Remarks and references to Appendices
M.25.b.5.2	Nov 12		40 Rounds fired at selected targets by Right Gun — difficult to observe in consequence of rapid fall of shells owing to the large of carrying parties.	See
	13		63 Rounds fired at selected targets by Right Guns — nothing by Left Guns.	See
	14		Battery relieved by 1st Canadian L.T.M.B. at 3-30 p.m. — Battery proceeded by tram to rest billets at GOUY SERVINS Q.35.d.0.6.	See
Q.35.d.0.6	15		Battery resting	See
Do	16		Do	See
J.35.c.5.0	17		Battery proceeded by Route march to HAUTEVILLE (J.35.c.5.0) Thence 51c	See
Do	18		Battery resting	See
h.2.c.5.0	19		Battery proceeded by Route March to RAULLENCOURT (h.2.c.5.0) Thence 57c	See
Do	20		Battery resting	See
G.13.b.8.7	21		Battery proceeded by Route march to Achiet le Petit (G.13.b.8.7) Thence 57c	See
W.2.c.5.0	22		Do to Achiet le Grand Thence to LESSART WOOD (W.2.c.5.0 while 57c)	See
Do	23		Firing by Trench Mortar Howitzer to LESSART WOOD	See
Do	24		Battery Training	See
Do	25		Do	See
Do	26		Do	See
E.13.c.1.5	27		Capt. Howard left Batty for an appointment at 1st Army School — Batty moved to TRESCAULT + Went into support for Hindenburg Line	Do

A5834 Wt.W4973/M687 750,000 8/16 D. D. & L. Ltd. Forms/C.2113/13.

MAP REFERENCE - SHEET FRANCE 57.

WAR DIARY
or
INTELLIGENCE SUMMARY

Army Form C. 2118.

of 177th Light Trench Mortar Batty.

NOVEMBER 1917

Place	Date	Hour	Summary of Events and Information	Remarks and references to Appendices
L-13-C-1-3	28		Battery moved to FLESQUIERES – Headquarters L.13.C.1.3. Dugouts taken over from 51st Guards Division.	A
	29		Battery had a day improving and extending dugouts – cleaning dugouts, including signs etc.	A
	30		Crew dug in around Battn. H.Q. at L.13.C.3.7. in spaces where old 177 TRENCHES supporting Regt. Front of the Trenches	A

James Dickinson Lieut
o/c 177th L.T.M.B.

Map Reference Sheet 57c France.   SECRET.

Army Form C. 2118.

WAR DIARY
or
INTELLIGENCE SUMMARY.
(Erase heading not required.)

of 177th Light Trench Mortar Battery

DECEMBER - 1917

Place	Date	Hour	Summary of Events and Information	Remarks and references to Appendices
Moeuvres L.13.c.1.3	1		2 guns dug in in support of 2/5 Lincoln Regt. at K.17.d.90.45 — Battery occupied this position during stand to at dusk.	
D°	2		Battery occupied Gun Positions	
D°	3		D°	
D°	4		D°	
K.29.d.1.6	5	3.0pm	Enemy advanced on our line from a direction of ORIVAL WOOD & GRAINCOURT - ANNEUX and were reported to SUGAR FACTORY at L.13.c.7.9. Lewis Guns on Right Flank (L.13.c.5.7) opened fire, firing about 90 rounds and attaining such hits among the enemy. The firing caused the enemy to retire and dig himself in out of range of these guns. Upon our line being faintly slightly forward these guns were put in new positions, when they could put down an effective barrage in front of our own line and also barrage our own front line, in case of the enemy temporarily holding that line. — Battery was relieved at night by the 178th L.T.M.B. and the Bn establishment at K.29.d.1.6 Battery resting at K.29.d.1.6.	
	6			
	7			
	8			
	9			
	10			
	11			
	12			
	13			
	14			

Map Reference Sheet 57c France
5/6

SECRET.

Army Form C. 2118.

WAR DIARY
of 177th Light Trench Mortar Battery

INTELLIGENCE SUMMARY.

(Erase heading not required.)

December 1917

Place	Date	Hour	Summary of Events and Information	Remarks and references to Appendices
K.29.d.1.6.	15		Battery Position at K.29.d.1.6.	
Do.	16		Do.	
FLESQUIERES	17		Battery Relieved 178th L.T.M.B. in the FLESQUIERES SECTOR	
Do	18		T.M. activity nil	
Do	19		Do	
Do	20		Do	
Do	21		Do	
Do	22		Battery Relieved by the 52nd L.T.M.B. - Spent night in HAVRINCOURT	
HAVRINCOURT	23		Battery proceeded by Route March to ROCQUIGNY	
ROCQUIGNY	24		Battery Resting	
RAMBRINES	25		Battery proceeded by march route to BAPAUME - entrained at 10.0 a.m. detrained at 2.30pm and marched KAMBRINES. Hd Qrs. I-3-C-0-5.	Sketch 57C
KAMBRINES	26		Battery cleaning & reorganising	
Do	27		Do	
Do	28		Battery Training	
Do	29		Do	
Do	30		CHURCH PARADE	
Do	31		Battery Training	

James Dickinson Captain
OC 177th L.T.M.B.

Map References France Sheet 51C

SECRET

Army Form C. 2118.

WAR DIARY
or
INTELLIGENCE SUMMARY

of 177th Light Trench Mortar Battery

JANUARY 1918

(Erase heading not required.)

Instructions regarding War Diaries and Intelligence Summaries are contained in F. S. Regs., Part II. and the Staff Manual respectively. Title pages will be prepared in manuscript.

Place	Date	Hour	Summary of Events and Information	Remarks and references to Appendices
APPRINES L.3.C.0.15	1		Battery Training — afternoon Recreational Training	
	2		Do	
	3		Do	
	4		Do	
	5		Do	
	6		Church Parade.	
	7		Battery Training — afternoon Recreational Training	
	8		Do	
	9		Do	
	10		Do	
	11		Do	
	12		Do	
	13		Church Parade.	
	14		Battery Training — afternoon Recreational Training	
	15		Do	
	16		Do	
	17		Do	
	18		Do	
	19		Do	
	20		Church Parade.	
	21		Battery Training — afternoon Recreational Training	
	22		Do	

Map Reference, France, Sheet 51c.

SECRET

WAR DIARY
— of — 177th Light Trench Mortar Battery
INTELLIGENCE SUMMARY.
JANUARY — 1918

Army Form C. 2118.

Instructions regarding War Diaries and Intelligence Summaries are contained in F.S. Regs., Part II. and the Staff Manual respectively. Title pages will be prepared in manuscript.

(Erase heading not required.)

Place	Date	Hour	Summary of Events and Information	Remarks and references to Appendices
AMBRINES	23		Battery Training — Afternoon Recreational Training	JR
T.3.c.0.5.	24		" 1.30 "	JR
	25		" 1.30 "	JR
	26		" 1.30 "	JR
	27		Church Parade	JR
	28		Battery Training — Afternoon Recreational Training	JR
	29		" 1.30 "	JR
	30		" 1.30 "	JR
	31		" 1.30 "	JR

James D. Robinson Captain
177th L.T.M.B.

[Stamp: 177TH LIGHT TRENCH MORTAR BATTERY 31-1-18]

SECRET

Army Form C. 2118.

WAR DIARY

of A/177th Light Trench Mortar Battery

INTELLIGENCE SUMMARY.

(Erase heading not required.)

February – 1918.

Instructions regarding War Diaries and Intelligence Summaries are contained in F. S. Regs., Part II. and the Staff Manual respectively. Title pages will be prepared in manuscript.

Map References { France 51c } Do 57c N.W.

Place	Date	Hour	Summary of Events and Information	Remarks and references to Appendices
AMBRINES	1		Battery Training – Afternoon Football Recreational Training	
	2		Do	
	3		Church Parade	
I.3.c.0.5.	4		Battery Training – Afternoon Football etc.	
	5		Inspection by Corps Commander.	
	6		Battery Training. Firing on Musketry Range in afternoon.	
	7		Battery Training. Afternoon Recreational Training.	
	8		Do	
P.24.d.2.7.	9		Battery proceeded by march route to GOUY-in-ARTOIS (Map reference R.24.d.2.7. Sheet 51c) Billeted there for the night.	
X.10.b.4.8.	10		Battery proceeded by march Route to BLAIREVILLE. (Map reference X.10.b.4.8. Sheet 51c) Billeted for one night.	
A.5.b.4.5.25.	11		Battery proceeded by march Route to HAMELINCOURT. (Map reference A.5.b.4.5.25. Sheet 57c N.W) Billeted for one night.	
B.17.c.5.5.	12		Battery relieved the 121st L.T.M.B. in the BULLÉCOURT SECTOR of the line. Relief carried out successfully. Headquarters established at B.17.c.5.5. Sheet 57c N.W.	
	13		No French Mortar Activity	

SECRET

WAR DIARY
of 177th Light Trench Mortar Battery
INTELLIGENCE SUMMARY
(Erase heading not required.)

Army Form C. 2118.

Map References France 51C
Do 57C N.W.

February 1918

Place	Date	Hour	Summary of Events and Information	Remarks and references to Appendices
B.17.b.5.5.	14		Our T.M's fired in Retaliation to Enemy T.Ms. on BUNNY HUG TRENCH + SAP HEAD at U.22.d.9.8. About 80 rounds were expended, the majority falling in the trench.	
	15		T.Ms fired on BUNNY HUG TRENCH + SAPHEAD at U.22.d.9.8. About 20 rounds being expended.	
	16		About 50 rounds were fired at the same targets.	
	17		No T.M. Activity	
	18		Do	
	19		Do	
	20		Do	
	21		Do	
	22		Do	
	23		T.M's fired 30 rounds on BUNNY HUG TRENCH + SAP HEAD at U.22.d.9.8.	
	24		No T.M. Activity	
	25		Do	
	26		20 rounds fired at BUNNY HUG TRENCH + SAP HEAD at U.22.d.9.8.	
	27		No T.M. activity	
	28		No T.M. activity	

James Wickinson
Captain O/C
177th L.T.M.B.

SECRET.

Headquarters
59 Division

[Stamp: HEADQUARTERS 177th INFANTRY BRIGADE No. 886/AQ 11 APR 1918]

Forwarded

11.4.18

H Gorley ?
Staff Captain for
Brig Genl Commdg
177th Infty Bde

MAP REFERENCES 57d N.W. FRANCE. SECRET.

Army Form C. 2118.

WAR DIARY of 177th Light Trench Mortar Battery

INTELLIGENCE SUMMARY

(Erase heading not required.)

March 1918.

Place	Date	Summary of Events and Information	Remarks and References to Appendices
B.17.b.55.	1	T.M activity Normal	
"	2	do	
"	3	do	
"	4	do	
"	5	do	
"	6	do	
"	7	do	
"	8	do	
"	9	do	
"	10	No. 1 + 2 Guns Registered on new S.O.S. Lines – 12 Rounds fired on No. 11 Target	
"	11	Hd. Qrs. moved to C.8.a.25.15. – No T.M activity.	
C.8.a.25.15.	12	No T.M. activity.	
"	13	Harassing fire on prepared shell holes in conjunction with Artillery.	
"	14	– No T.M. activity	
"	15	18 Rounds fired on newly camouflaged gun pit.	
"	16	50 Rounds fired in support of party sent out to rescue a wounded man.	
"	17	No T.M activity	
"	18	ditto	
"	19	2 Guns fired for 15 Minutes in support of a Bombing Raid. Excellent result obtained. – Battery relieved in the line by the 176th L.T.M.B.	
MORY.	20	Battery Resting.	

MAP REFERENCES: FRANCE 57° N.W.

"SECRET."
Army Form C. 2118.

WAR DIARY
or
INTELLIGENCE SUMMARY.
(Erase heading not required.)

of 177th Field Trench Mortar Battery

MARCH - 1918.

Place	Date	Hour	Summary of Events and Information	Remarks and References to Appendices
N/DRY	21	7·0 A.M.	Battery moved up in support of Division - Brigade formed up between VAUX-VRAUCOURT and HOMME MORT	
		7·40 A.M.	2/Lieut. G.H. Sutherland and 2 teams detailed to 2/5 Lincs - 2/Lieut. J. Vincent & 2 teams to 2/4 Leicester Regt. - The remaining 3 guns were held in reserve on the VAUX - MORY Road.	
		12 NOON	Orders received for 2/5 Lincs and 2/4 Leicesters to move forward - Guns went with respective Battalions and acted under direct orders of Battalion O.C. concerned. Took up positions to cover their front. Carried forward ammunition from nearest available Dumps - The 3 remaining guns moved forward and the	
		1·0 P.M.	4th London Regt. took up position 500 yards E of VAUX SUGAR FACTORY. Their guns were swung in pits. Small sangars and fully hid. Their camouflaged, made, and put on pits - Ammunition rapidly replaced in pits and the batteries - Ammunition rapidly replaced in pits and the batteries	
		1·3 P.M.	O.C. 176" L.T.M.B. reported to our new arrangement to cover L/f flank making 3 camouflaged road with his 3 remaining guns - during evening fighting in front (W) of ECOUST. 2/Lieut. G.H. Sutherland +5 ORs were evacuated, the	SJ
2/22		4·0 P.M.	former being killed. L/corpr. Bliss acting Bn. sjt. by 120 Bde. Command withdrew the night to support the withdrawal of the infantry. Came in contact with the enemy attached from ECOUST and passed over our front line. The A.T.S. Regd. kept on withdrew without from our front line.	
		4·20 P.M.	3 Guns in position + their teams dug up in steady line along camouflaged road and was in fact the - Visible orders from O.C. 4th Leicester that infantry were retiring to reorganise - 3 Guns took up a stand fire and covered the retirement of infantry - Ammunition in use rapidly in knocks/parcels to the	
		11·35 P.M.	3rd Northern Battery dumps... Shells and ammt - for men had in telling order took up position as in party in support	SJ

"SECRET"

Army Form C. 2118.

MAP REFERENCES: FRANCE 57c N.W.

Instructions regarding War Diaries and Intelligence Summaries are contained in F. S. Regs, Part II. and the Staff Manual respectively. Title pages will be prepared in manuscript.

WAR DIARY (CONTINUED)
of 177th Light Trench Mortar Battery
INTELLIGENCE SUMMARY

(Erase heading not required.)

MARCH 1918

PLACE	DATE	HOUR	Summary of Events and Information	Remarks and References to Appendices
MORY	21/22	11.30pm	The troops of the 120th & 119th Bdes. who still held our front line – Guard End N–established in the outposts	JR
		3.0pm	Bosche seen advancing to VAUX VRAUCOURT	
		5.15pm	Snipers into our men from VAUX outskirts	
VAUX VRAUCOURT	22	5.30pm	Infantry on right flanks all withdrawn – VAUX VRAUCOURT in hands of enemy – Enfilading our right – sniping – sweeping M.G. fire from rear. About dusk General withdrawal to Army Line ordered – arrived at under fire, Heavy M.G. & Sniper fire. – Arrived at Beugnâtre – remaining guns despatched to Q.M. Stores at	JR
		8.0pm	To act as riflemen. After dusk parties from thereouts went to Bapaume (Verbal) to withdrew to AVREPS – BAPAUME road Low Est. 50 & 4'' finns when and the Brigade was forming up to reorganise on man's road. Captain Withenshaw served on parties wherever enemy to Brigade, when meeting with him came in	
		9.0pm	from between S of MORY and M.N. of BEUGNATRE	
	22/23	12midnight	Depot deposition our sunken Road along track from MORY to ACHAGNIES	
		6.0am	arriving MORY + E.61 MORY. All night fighting. Hands were in village under any from M.G. fire – Casualties NIL	
		6.30pm	Reported to re # Lancashire – held in reserve in Trenches behind the Front. – Very snipers from trench fairly quiet. – Our artillery shooting very light all day.	
	24	8.0pm	Reported attack by enemy on LT FUSILIERS – our left flank N.E. of FUSILIERS – Lewis S.O.S. went up – Sent out Kreuzel parties will prospects to cover the valley TRENCH RES. Heavy M.G. & rifle fire were Artillery – own troops to S.O.S. movements reported to be most numerous	JR

References: 57.C.N.W FRANCE

"SECRET"
Army Form C. 2118.

WAR DIARY (CONTINUED)
of 177th Light Trench Mortar Battery

INTELLIGENCE SUMMARY

March - 1918

PLACE	DATE	HOUR	Summary of Events and Information	Remarks and References to Appendices
BEHAGNIES	24/25	12 midn't	Interviewed O.C. 4th Lincolns and found out situation — brought Battery to B.H.Q. and asked to act if necessary as "stiffening" Troops to E. Surreys & R.W. Kents — not called upon	X
	25	Dawn	"Stood to" but nothing unusual took place	
		12 noon	Right Flank Troops saw nothing — 6 camels of machines reported back town — broke through on Right — took no action — having right flank in conjunction with R.E.'s. 59th Bn M.G.C. & R.S.F.'s. Special reports frequently which BEHAGNIES settled our troops were in advance	XX
		2:30pm	Our Artillery shelled BEHAGNIES	
		3:0pm	General retirement of Divisions on our Right — leaving om. G. Bullets came from our ridge BEHAGNIES — SAPIGNIES	
		3:30pm	Our own fire too low without to take ERVILLERS — BEHAGNIES ridge — too hot of position on various slopes of ridge running up to MARIECOURT to protect him after Instructed to withdraw behind GOMMECOURT to cover our retreat of infantry M.G. being left behind to cover our withdrawal.	
		4:0pm	Lost our Lewis with 172 Brigade — Reported to G.O.C. 173 L.F. & 5th Lg in in Railway embankment	
		6:30pm	Made repeated attempts to gain touch with 4th Lincolns without success — report received they had been shelled and spilled. Our own Barrage GOMMECOURT — a.m. to 1830 function and railway	
25/26		2:30 am	M.G. Bullets first direction of ACHIET LE GRAND	XXX
	26	midn't	Brigade retired in light of E. Lances 46 — marched to BIHUCOURT	
		6am	Marched to FONQUEVILLERS	
		&c 5:30pm	Stood to on SAILLY Road — BIENVILLERS — Billets for the night	

Map References 57D N.W. France.

March 1918.

Army Form C. 2118.

WAR DIARY (continued)
of 177th Light French Mortar Battery
INTELLIGENCE SUMMARY

"SECRET"

(Erase heading not required.)

PLACE	DATE	HOUR	Summary of Events and Information	Remarks and References to Appendices
Sus St. Leger	27	9.0 am	Marched to Sus St Leger	
	28		Billets in Sus St Leger — 14 hrs relieving stores offload — Ayette abandoned.	
Beugin	29	6.30 pm	Marched to Frevent — Entrained to Houdain	
	30	5.0 am	Arrived and billetted at Beugin	
	31	10.30 am	Inspection by G.O.C. 59th Division	

177TH LIGHT TRENCH MORTAR BATTERY.
No. ....
Date ...2-4-18

James Watkins
Captain
OC 177th L.T.M.B.

Map Reference:- "Lens" Locre.
28 Belgium & France.

WAR DIARY
of the 177th Light Trench Mortar Battery
INTELLIGENCE SUMMARY
APRIL – 1918

(Erase heading not required.)

Army Form C. 2118.

Place	Date	Hour Time	Summary of Events and Information	Remarks and references to Appendices
BEUGIN	1	1.0 pm	Entrained for PROVEN.	
SCHOOL CAMP	2	9.30 am	Armed School Camp (between WATOU & Poperinghe).	
Do	3		Bailey Carrying up Carpets.	
Do	4		Brigade inspected by G.O.C. 2nd Army.	
I.3.6.8.2	5		Battery proceeded by light Railway to line relieved 100/27 mtrs Headquarters at Abeural Camp (I.3.6.8.3).	
Do	6		no movement	
Do	7		Do	
Do	8		Do	
Do	9		Do	
Do	10		Do	
St Josephs Institute	11		Bde. Qrs moved to ST JOSEPHS INSTITUTE.	
Brandhoek	12		Battery withdrawn from Line - Billetted at Brandhoek	
Do	13	2.0 pm	Battery entrained for GODEWAERSVELDE - Resettlement for night at MONT des CATS in Monastery.	
MONT des CATS	14	3.0 pm	Battery proceeded by Route March to LOCRE.	

Map Reference "Lens"
28 Belgium & France

"Scout"
Mr. J.L.R.... Montabetty
APRIL 1918.

WAR DIARY
INTELLIGENCE SUMMARY
Army Form C. 2118.

(Erase heading not required.)

Place	Date	Hour	Summary of Events and Information	Remarks and references to Appendices
LOCRE	15		Battery standing by — Headquarters moved to Eradic Camp owing to being heavily shelled.	
Eradic Camp	16		Battery standing by	
do	17		Battery turned into Shelters and pack-movements - Brigades HQ 74 Punjabis Regt in support	
do	18		Bths	
Ringhelst	19		Brigade relieved by French troops, moved back to Ringhelst & billetted for one night there	
do	20		Battery proceeded by Route March to 2nd Bucket Camp BAM BECQUE	
BAM BECQUE	21		Battery Resting and Cleaning up	
do	22		do	
do	23		Training — of various Provisional Parties	
do	24		do	
do	25		do	
do	26		do	

"SECRET."

Maps/Sheets: LENS. 11. BELGIUM & FRANCE
Sheet 27 BELGIUM & FRANCE
27NE
27 NW BELGIUM

Army Form C. 2118.

WAR DIARY

of 177th Light Trench Mortar Battery

INTELLIGENCE SUMMARY.

(Erase heading not required.)

APRIL 1918

Instructions regarding War Diaries and Intelligence Summaries are contained in F.S. Regs., Part II. and the Staff Manual respectively. Title pages will be prepared in manuscript.

Hour, Date, Place	Summary of Events and Information	Remarks and references to Appendices
BAMBECQUE 27.	Battery moved to School Camp — Entrained 6:30pm	A1
School Camp 28.	" to L.29.b.8.2. — Camp shelter trench	A1
L.29.b.8.2. 29	Actively carrying ammunition — Hy. B. moved to G.26.c.35.50 (Sheet 28.NW) enemy shelling.	A1
G.26.c.35.50 30	A Gun Position dug up Support lines. Gunners & guns ammunition moved to replaced	A1

Francis Dickinson Capt
OC 177 LTMB.

Sheet 28 N.W. Belgium "Secret"
No. 177. 2" Light Trench Mortar Battery
Army Form C. 2118.

WAR DIARY
INTELLIGENCE SUMMARY

May 1918

Place	Date	Hour	Summary of Events and Information	Remarks and references to Appendices
	1		Maintaining.	
G.26.c.35.w.	2		Guns manned in Eastfortnight line.	
do.	3		Disposition guns in support line.	
do.	4		New position Dug. Ammunitions prepared.	
Hoetaque	5		Battery withdrawn from support line. Billets in Hoetaque.	
do.	6		Aeroplane at night. Battery proceeded by Busses to St. Momelin Area.	
	7		Battery resting	
	8		provided by trains to base. — Battery entrained	

Lawson Stokgner
Captain
O.C. 177 LTMB

WAR DIARY
or
INTELLIGENCE SUMMARY.

Army Form C. 2118.

177th Trench Mortar Battery

AUGUST 1918

17th to 31st

WAR DIARY
or
INTELLIGENCE SUMMARY.

(Erase heading not required.)

Army Form C. 2118.

Place	Date	Hour	Summary of Events and Information	Remarks and references to Appendices
BARLY	August 17		Training	
do	18	5.30 a.m	Marched to GOUY-EN-ARTOIS	
GOUY		7 p.m	Entrained for BLAIRVILLE	
BLAIRVILLE		(?) p.m	Disposed at do	
do		9/-	Report 19 R.I.T.M.B. in reserve on Hypothesis when un-position	
			2 Guns at TNB C.8.3.4 covering Railway from S.12.a.0.1. to S.11.b.1	
			1 Gun at D.1.b.1.0 swamp & roads at S.10. & 8.6	
			1 Gun at D.1.b.1.5 to C.19 communications BOISLEUX AU SUD from N.14.a.5.9 to	
			S. & G. 5 the	
			2 Guns at M.31 d. F.3 covering road M.6.29.49 and N.31.b.45	
			to communications BLAIRVILLE BOISRY	
			old gun Emplacements improved but not considered	
L.N.E.	19		to be bullet proof.	
do	20	6 p.m	Newly(?) erected wall H.E. Shells and for cases	
do	21	12.30	2 Guns from support to S.6.c.3.4. in return to N.B. D.L.I.	
			in relieving post at Sud at S.6.b.2.7 and N.34.c.7.3	
do		5.30	20 scouts fired on + ask if all O.K. Henry M.G. (pult) go out from S.6.d.7.2 to road	
			of Guns and Lys on left and one M.G. (pult) go cont from S.6.d.7.2 to road	
			covering 2 O.R's on return to duty 9 a/c W.G. Scott(?)	3 O.R's wounded
			and M. Railway Bridge near S.6.0.10	

Army Form C. 2118.

WAR DIARY
or
INTELLIGENCE SUMMARY.

(Erase heading not required.)

Instructions regarding War Diaries and Intelligence Summaries are contained in F.S. Regs., Part II and the Staff Manual respectively. Title pages will be prepared in manuscript.

Place	Date	Hour	Summary of Events and Information	Remarks and references to Appendices
	AUGUST			
F. LINE	22	1 pm	[illegible] and 100 [illegible] round from support & S.H. Sec in number 2/6 & D.L.I in enemy posn at S 3, 2 & 9.A. and [illegible] reported	JC
		5 pm	been going on there	JC
LINE	23	12.50 am 5.30 pm	Heavy gas shelling of positions at S 3, 4, 9, 1, 5 and S.11.9. 27 and m.25	JC JC
BLAIRVILLE		5.30 am	All quiet withdrawn from the line and concentrated at BLAIRVILLE – 9.11.93	JC
			N.C.Os all foregoing night reported ate from SHEET 51. 6.5N. ELSE.	
			Battn marched to SAULTY	
la		3 pm	Arrived at SAULTY	JR
SAULTY	24	7	Entrained for AIRE	JR
do		8 pm	Detained [illegible] do	JR
AIRE		12 m midnight	Marched to LAMBRES	JR
			Billeting	JR
LAMBRES	25	1 am	Embused for ST VENANT	JR
do	26		do	JR
ST VENANT		3 pm	Debussed at [illegible]	JR
	27	4.30 am	[illegible] 220th I. M. Bn— at Q.9.a7. P.24.d.45. my [illegible] any H	JC
			Ban, at Rollans 2 Beyn at K 35.d.69. 2 Coms. at Q 10. 232	
			each H Bain in Reserve at P 24.d.75	

Army Form C. 2118.

WAR DIARY
or
INTELLIGENCE SUMMARY.
(Erase heading not required.)

Instructions regarding War Diaries and Intelligence Summaries are contained in F. S. Regs., Part II. and the Staff Manual respectively. Title pages will be prepared in manuscript.

Place	Date	Hour	Summary of Events and Information	Remarks and references to Appendices
FRONT LINE	28		[illegible]	
		11 am	About 30 5.9 shells fell round [illegible] but caused damage in [illegible]	
do	29		Our [illegible] still upon	
			Pockets [illegible] shelled with 5.9 and 4.2 [illegible]	
do			[illegible] Pockets in [illegible]	
do	30	3 pm	Our Guns and Front Line J.35.d.5.1 in [illegible]	
			5.C. Guns and sim bombs at L.31.c.9.5 with 150 rounds	
			[illegible] and [illegible] intelligence	
			LETTER [illegible]	
do			[illegible] Infantry taking over Line 22 [illegible] K	
			Our guns taken over by [illegible] L.10.c.5.4	
CALONNE	31		N.B. All map references are 28 & map sheet from 1/20,000	
			VIEILLE CHAPELLE BETHUNE	

WAR DIARY
or
INTELLIGENCE SUMMARY.

Army Form C. 2118.

177th Trench Mortar Battery

September 1918

2.10.18

Army Form C. 2118.

WAR DIARY
or
INTELLIGENCE SUMMARY.
(Erase heading not required.)

Instructions regarding War Diaries and Intelligence Summaries are contained in F.S. Regs., Part II. and the Staff Manual respectively. Title pages will be prepared in manuscript.

Place	Date	Hour	Summary of Events and Information	Remarks and references to Appendices
CALONNE	Aug 1	4pm	Battery moved to K.9.c.6.8.	
			1 O.R. wounded in action	
LESTREM	2	9am	Reconnaissance and arrangements made to draw two guns with each Battalion out of action during the attack	
do		3pm	Battery relieved by 198th T.M.B and 3 guns to support at Q.14.c.9.6	
			and guns withdrawn by 196th T.M.B at full fire and thence marched	
CALONNE	3	3pm	Battery arrived at ST VENANT	
ST VENANT	4	5.15pm	Arrived at Hospital ST VENANT	
do	5	Noon	Remainder of CALONNE	
			Strength of CALONNE and needed to PARADIS Q.12.e.5.0	
			together ready to B. today to complete establishment. Guns arrived last night	
PARADIS	6			
	7	3pm	Moved to LESTREM R.15.d.35.75 arriving at 4.30 p.m.	
LESTREM	8		Testing	
do	9	6am	Relieved by M.14.b.89 relieved 196th T.M.B in Coys Main Battle line between	
do	10		M.9.c.3.0 and B.33.a.0.50 Battn Battle line and outpost positions for transferring Coys March Battn Hqrs. B Bank, N. Engine	
do	11	9.1.2	Copying & Entrances from Guards: 1 at M.9.c.2.3: 1 at M.9.d.3.6: 1 at M.9.d.3.8 all covering right flank. BATTERS POST the two covering Right flank; Gun to Battery writing 2nd gun to the Hazel Forage.	

Instructions regarding War Diaries and Intelligence Summaries are contained in F. S. Regs., Part II. and the Staff Manual respectively. Title pages will be prepared in manuscript.

WAR DIARY
or
INTELLIGENCE SUMMARY.
(Erase heading not required.)

I/2

Army Form C. 2118.

Place	Date	Hour	Summary of Events and Information	Remarks and references to Appendices
LESTREM	11/9/18		and positions for 4 Guns; one at M 8 b 30.20; one at M 2 b 30.40; one at G 32 d 5.7, and one at G 32 d 4.7; the 4 Guns covering left Bn front. 2/Lt W.G. Scott struck off strength – Gassed – Base List No 1677 and granted 3 weeks leave to U. Kingdom.	–
CORPS MAIN BATTLE LINE	12	All day	Same as 11th. The following promotions are approved by G.O.C. 177th Inf. Bde with effect from 12-9-18:– No 351921 Cpl Kendall T. 2/6th D.L.I. to be Sergt. " 17857 L/Cpl Lee G.W. 1/5th S.L.I " " Corp. " 3369 Pte Rendall C. do. " " L/Cpl. " 302526 L/C. Mackey F.J.W. 2/6th D.L.I " " Cpl. " 350350 " Middleton J.W. 15th Essex Regt " Cpl. " 55649 " Huggett R. do " " Cpl. " 25216 Pte Rushton A.J. do " " L/Cpl. (Paid) " 49365 " Dickinson ? 11th S.L.I " " L/Cpl. (Paid) The following N.C.Os returned to Unit as unsuitable for T.M.B. No 55538 Corp. Barton A.J. } 15th Essex Regt. " 35732 L/Cpl Smith A.D. }	All map references to sheet VIEILLE CHAPELLE 36 S.E.
	13	10pm	Relieved 176th T.M.B. whose dispositions were as follows:– H.Q. M 11 c 5.6 (AUBERS 36 S.W.1); two Guns on Right Bn. front; one at N 7 c 9.2, and one at N 1 a 85.35 4 Guns in Reserve at Battery H.Q. Shelled on and off all night at Battery H.Q.	All map references from sheet AUBERS 36 S.W. 1
	14		" " " " day with H.E. & Gas Shells at Battery H.Q.	

D. D. & L., London, E.C.
(10340) Wt W5300/P713 750,000 3/18 Forms/C2118/16.

Army Form C. 2118.

WAR DIARY
or
INTELLIGENCE SUMMARY.
(Erase heading not required.)

Instructions regarding War Diaries and Intelligence Summaries are contained in F. S. Regs., Part II. and the Staff Manual respectively. Title pages will be prepared in manuscript.

Place	Date	Hour	Summary of Events and Information	Remarks and references to Appendices
LINE	14	1/pm	10 Rds fired at TWO TREE FARM. Small parties of enemy seem to have very nebulous no retaliation.	MM
"	15	12.15pm	Carrying on with the retaliation. 25 rds fired at THE COTTAGE N.7.d.55.50 and twice on Rgt same point.	MM
			10 rds fired at N.7.d.95.66 firing was carried out in conjunction with an M.G. of 11th S.L.I.	
			9.10 rds 5ths Master Ammunition. Fired from Cross Roads on M.16.d to the Battalion Front on new emplacement at N.7.e.90.20	MM
	16	1.45am	and continued on new emplacement at N.7.c.90.20	
			25 rds fired at trench junction N.7.d. 15.25 where enemy M.G. was firing. 10 rds had been fired from one T.M. that M.G. ceased firing & did not fire again all night - in all probability it was knocked out.	
			Completing Emplacements + Carrying Ammunition, see diary.	MM
	17			
	18	1am	30 was fired at enemy M.G. N.I.a.92.30. + M.G. put out of action & enemy killed.	
			6 rds were then fired at retiring enemy affecting casualties on enemy.	
		6.30am	24 rds fired at TWO TREE FARM and casualties inflicted on enemy.	
		8.30—	20 rds fired at JOCKS LODGE N.7.&.5.3.	
		1.15—	15 rds fired at enemy M.G. N.13.c.8.3. when M.G. ceased firing.	
		1.20—	10 was fired at enemy M.G. Post. N.I.c.8.1.	
	19		11 rds fired at TWO TREES FARM.	
			Carrying Ammunition	
		11pm	3 guns were in position for operation against TWO TREE FARM but operation cancelled.	

WAR DIARY
or
INTELLIGENCE SUMMARY.

(Erase heading not required.)

Army Form C. 2118.

Place	Date SEPT	Hour	Summary of Events and Information	Remarks and references to Appendices
LINE	20	4.20pm	all quiet. Carrying ammunition?	
	21		50 rds fired on each of following points N.1.c.8.1. N.1.2.8.5. N.7.6.4.5.20	
			Fairly heavy retaliation, but no casualties	
	22		Relieved by 178th T.M.B. Relief completed 10 p.m. Marched back to Div	
			Reserve. LA BASSEE – ESTAIRS Rd. 6 Guns in position protecting certain points	
			on Corps Main Battle Line.	
	23		Cleaning up.	
	24		Training	
	25		do	
	26		do	
	27		do Bn.H.M. 15 minutes L.I. practice Explains the attack on 17th Sept. 18	
	28		Recon. Party Div. for position in connection with attack of 19.77.77 on 3 Guns in 3.2	
	29		Cleaning detraining weapons	
			L.M. 75 mins of indirect work.	
	30	7pm	300 rounds fired on Enemy front line.	
			1 Gun had 2 premature casualties M. Firing casualties.	
			2/Lt. BABBIDGE wounded	
			402085 L/Cpl Pickworth " S.L.I. killed	
			402157 " PE ROTHE H/ " do	
			4.22.57 " JONES A.W " do	
			4.20.77 " HOLT F. " do	
			4.20.49	

Army Form C. 2118.

WAR DIARY
INTELLIGENCE SUMMARY.

(Erase heading not required.)

Instructions regarding War Diaries and Intelligence Summaries are contained in F. S. Regs., Part II. and the Staff Manual respectively. Title pages will be prepared in manuscript.

179th Trench Mortar Battery

October, 1918

Place	Date	Hour	Summary of Events and Information	Remarks and references to Appendices

WAR DIARY
INTELLIGENCE SUMMARY.

Army Form C. 2118.

Place	Date	Hour	Summary of Events and Information	Remarks and references to Appendices
LINE	Oct 1		No firing.	
			No. 30252 6 Cpl MACKEY. P.T.M. Wounded in Action.	
			2/Lt W.E. SCOTT reported for duty from sick leave to U.K.	
			The following men posted to M.Battery to complete Establishment & replace casualties:-	
			No. 18372 Pte DICKINSON H.C. 11th Somerset L.I.	
			" 266027 " WALKER W. "	
			" 262252 " KEETON R. "	
			" 18383 " BOLLEM C. "	
			" 401260 " CHAPMAN R. 15th Essex Regt.	
	Oct 2	7.30am	50 rounds fired in conjunction with operation by 176th Bde on TWO TREE FARM. Retired in Line by 14th T.M.B. & marched back to LA BASSEE Rd.	
	Oct 3	2pm	Battery marched to SAILLY and into fresh billets.	
			No. 80349 Pte GODDARD G.W. Struck off Strength (Sick)	
			2 Guns & teams attached to 2/6 DURHAM L.I. in LINE.	
	4		No. 55849 Cpl HUGGETT. R. returned from leave to U.K.	
	5		2 Guns attached to 1A SOMERSET L.I. in Line	
	6	2pm	Remainder of Battery marched to BOIS GRENIER.	
		6.45am	80 rounds fired at I.34.d.3.4 and I.34.b.3.2	
			No. 25780-9 Pte JACKSON. T.W. 2/6 D.L.I. Promoted L/Cpl w/effect from 1.10.18	
			No. 18290 TIMBRELL E.W. 11th Somerset L.I.	
			No. 55815 Pte RAINE. T. 15th Essex Regt. Accidentally injured and admitted to hospital	

Army Form C. 2118.

WAR DIARY
or
INTELLIGENCE SUMMARY.
(Erase heading not required.)

Instructions regarding War Diaries and Intelligence Summaries are contained in F. S. Regs., Part II. and the Staff Manual respectively. Title pages will be prepared in manuscript.

Place	Date	Hour	Summary of Events and Information	Remarks and references to Appendices
LINE	July 7		No firing	
	8		No firing	
			No. 79774 Pte STUDMAN R.S. (2/5 D.L.I) reported for duty following evening from wound (G.S.) from 55th General Hospital	
			Capt. A.T. COOK granted leave to U.K. from 6.10.18 to 25.11.15. 2/Lt D.B. HAINING assumed temporary command of Battery in his absence	
	9	15.30	16 rounds fired from I.34.a.7.8. at M.G. in FARM I.34.6.3.2. Several direct hits observed but result unknown	
	10		No firing. Before Scheme for Night Barrage Scheme & Barrage Front prepared and approved by G.O.C. 4 guns in position covering important grounds to wit:—	
			No 1 Gun at (I 33 c 7.6) covering cross country between ground (I 33 d 8.5.20)	
			No 2 Gun at (I 33 c 7.6)	
			No 3 " (I 27 b 05.10) (I 33 6 65.20)	
			No 4 " (I 27 a 95.50) roads junction at (I 26 c 6.0.45)	
	21.15		Battery relieved by 176th T.M.B.	
	22.25		Guns withdrawn to Brigade Reserve. FARM (I 26 c 2.4)	
FORT ROMPU	11		Reorganising m.t.	
	12		General Cleaning up	FORT ROMPU (N 6 a 75.45)

WAR DIARY
INTELLIGENCE SUMMARY
(Erase heading not required.)

Army Form C. 2118.

Instructions regarding War Diaries and Intelligence Summaries are contained in F. S. Regs., Part II. and the Staff Manual respectively. Title pages will be prepared in manuscript.

Place	Date	Hour	Summary of Events and Information	Remarks and references to Appendices
FORT ROMPU	Oct 13	15·00	Resting. Divisional Commander lectured unit officers.	a/c
"	14	8·30	Inspection & distribution of Passes by Corps Commander.	a/c
"	15		Training.	a/c
			Preparation of scheme for defence of Divisional frontline and selecting positions for 8 guns. Positions chosen on map ref:	
			No. I 9 h. I 31 a 4·5, 3·5 Crossing MILITARY ROAD in I 31 d	
			" 2 " I 31 a 2·5, 6·0 Crossing network of tracks and road I 31 d.	
			" 3 " H 30 af 9·0, 2·5 Crossing junction of C.T. and road I 25 a	
			" 4 " I 25 a 3·8 Crossing road running N.E. I 19 c & d.	
			" 5 " I 19 a 8·9 Crossing road and track running N.E. and S./middle I 19 f & d.	
			" 6 " I 13 c 8·1 Crossing junction of C.T. I 20 a 1·4.	
			" 7 " I 7 d 6·2 Crossing military C.T. I 8 a.	
			" 8 " I 7 d 5·2 Crossing track & again I 7 f & in I a 2	
			Scheme submitted to O/C 1st (G.O.C) Brigade	
"	16	14·00	Moved from FORT ROMPU (W 8 a 9·6) to BOIS GRENIER (H 29 k 6·2)	a/c
BOIS GRENIER	17	14·15	Moved from BOIS GRENIER (H 29 d 6·2) to MONT de PREMESQUES (I 30 a 7·4)	a/c
MONT de PREMESQUES	18	09·30	Moved from MONT de PREMESQUES (I 30 a 7·4) to LOMMELET (K 14 a 6·7)	a/c
		20·15	Moved from LOMMELET (K 14 a 8·7) to MONS en BAROEUL (K 3 5 f 4·2)	a/c
MONS en BAROEUL	19	13·00	Moved from MONS en BAROEUL (K 35 b 4·2) to L'HEMPONPONT (L 29 f 9·7)	Arrived HEMPONPONT 18·00 36 E.U.B
L'HEMPONPONT	20	15·40	Moved from L'HEMPONPONT (L 29 f 9·7) to WILLEMS (Q 5 d 9·5·35)	

WAR DIARY
INTELLIGENCE SUMMARY
(Erase heading not required.)

Army Form C. 2118.

Place	Date	Hour	Summary of Events and Information	Remarks and references to Appendices
WILLEMS	21		Resting	
"	22	9.30	Received orders to relieve 176th T.M.B. Presented to H20A 1.6.	
HULANS		18.00	Position reconnoitred for spare guns, and guns sent strain under Command of 2/Lt. W.E. SCOTT present to LINE (11.00 mm)	
LINE			No 1 Gun I 19 d 5.2 covering N. track from enemy entanglement (I 20 b 25)	
			" 2 " I 19 d 5.6 " " (I 20 c 4.7)	
			" 3 " I 19 b 6.6 road in I 20 a from batteries and wire tracks	
			" 4 " I 19 b 8.7 covering bridge all approaches I 14 d 2.2	
			In addition No 1 + 2 guns are available	
			50 rounds ready for use with each gun position if possible	
			S.O.S. signal	
"	23	16.45	Battery moved Headquarters from HULANS (H20b1.6) to (H29X.N.) Enemy position, no firing.	
"	24		No firing	
"	25	22.15	20 rounds fired at M.G. at I 27 b.7 from SUNKEN ROAD (I 26 A)	
			Exact result of shoot not known	
"	26		No firing	
"	27		No 175757 Capt. G.W. LEE awarded M.M. Gallantry in action II C.R.O 679 of 27.10.18	
			Bn Firing.	
"	28	21.15	20 rounds fired at TRACK between I 26 b 3.4 and I 26 b 9.8 from I 26 a 3.5. Enemy retaliated with M.G. and T.M.s.	

Army Form C. 2118.

WAR DIARY
INTELLIGENCE SUMMARY.
(Erase heading not required.)

Place	Date	Hour	Summary of Events and Information	Remarks and references to Appendices
LINE	29		No firing	
"	30	6.25	42 rounds fired m.M.G. at I.26.b.1.4 and along TRACK to I.26.b.9.5. M.G. ceased firing	
"		22 m	26 rounds fired from I.8.d.0.7 at E. Post. I.9.c.4.8 Enemy did not retaliate.	
"	31	18.30	12 rounds harassing fire on I.26 a + b.	
			Capt. A.J. Cook returned from leave to U.K. granted 5 days extension. Auth W.O. 2077/257.(A.G.4)	

CONFIDENTIAL

Army Form C. 2118.

WAR DIARY
INTELLIGENCE SUMMARY.
(Erase heading not required.)

Instructions regarding War Diaries and Intelligence Summaries are contained in F. S. Regs., Part II. and the Staff Manual respectively. Title pages will be prepared in manuscript.

Place	Date	Hour	Summary of Events and Information	Remarks and references to Appendices

197th Trench Mortar Battery

November, 1918

Army Form C. 2118.

17th L.T.M.B'y

Confidential

WAR DIARY
or
INTELLIGENCE SUMMARY

(Erase heading not required.)

Nov 1918

Instructions regarding War Diaries and Intelligence Summaries are contained in F.S. Regs., Part II. and the Staff Manual respectively. Title pages will be prepared in manuscript.

Place	Date	Hour	Summary of Events and Information	Remarks and references to Appendices
LINE	1.11.18	05.45	1/2 rounds fired on Tracks I.26.b.4.4 to I.26.b.8.8.	A.C.C. Reference SHEET 37. Ed. 3 Belgium & France
	2.		2/Lt C.A. GREGORY 15th Essex Regt attached to Battery for duty. No. 18322 Pte. DICKINSON. H. 11th Somerset L.I. Struck off strength. sick.	
		03.57 04.30	13.0 rounds fired on enemy posts in I.20.d. and I.28.b in conjunction with raid by 11th S.L.I. on CABT LIETARD	
	3.	11.00	No. 252576 L/Cpl RUSHTON. A.S. 15th Essex Regt Struck off strength. – sick 15 rounds fired at enemy posts I.26.a.8.5.	
	4.		No. 246255 Pte BOND. A.C. 11th S.L.I. rejoined Unit from Hospital.	
	5.×		15 rounds fired on Track I.26.b.1.4. No. 350,353 Pte SAUNDERS. H. 15th Essex Regt. attached to Battery	
	6.×	05.45	15 rounds fired at I.26.b.0.03 The following O.Rs attached for duty No. 357204 Pte ADAM. O. 15th Essex Regt" 557127 O'DONOGHUE.T. do I.26.a. 252442 " HALL L. 2/5th D.L.I.	
	7.	05.30	20 rounds fired on Track No. 18405 Pte STONES.W.) 11th S.L.I. attached for duty. 265117 HARVEY.C.)	
	8.	00.03 05.30	1/19 rounds fired on tracks through enemy march I.20.a. 50 rounds fired on enemy posts in I.26.b & Railway I.9.2	

Army Form C. 2118.

WAR DIARY
INTELLIGENCE SUMMARY.
(Erase heading not required.)

2 Nov. 1918

Place	Date	Hour	Summary of Events and Information	Remarks and references to Appendices
LINE	8	18.00	Relieved by 178th T.M.B. and Battery marched back to TOUFFLEERS.	
	9		No. 2440 & 48 7 Pte. SMITH L. 2/6th D.L.I. attached to Battery.	
			Resting at TOUFFLEERS.	
	10		No. 252418 Pte CARRODUS V. granted 14 days special leave to U.K.	
	11	11.00	Battery marched to ESQUELMES.	
		15.00	Hostilities ceased.	
	12		Battery marched to TEMPLEUVE.	
	13		Resting. Training.	
	14		No. 243/644 Pte RICE P.E. 2/6 D.L.I. struck off strength — sick.	
			266034 " WADE W. 11th S.L.I. do do	
	15	08.20	March to PONT à TRESSIN and moved there at 14.00.	
	16	09.00	SECLIN and arrived there at 14.30.	
SECLIN	17		Resting	
	18		Training	
			2/Lt C.A. GREGORY 15th Essex Regt. posted to Battery vice 2/Lt T.P.R. RABBIDGE 15th Essex Regt. evacuated in autumn.	
	19		2/Lt W.E. SCOTT, 4/6th D.L.I. posted to Battery vice return from sick leave to U.K.	

Army Form C. 2118.

177th A.A. T.M. Bty

Confidential

3 Nov. 1918

WAR DIARY
INTELLIGENCE SUMMARY.
(Erase heading not required.)

Place	Date	Hour	Summary of Events and Information	Remarks and references to Appendices
SECLIN	19		Commenced Educational Training.	
	20		Educational Training	
	21		do	
	22		do	
	23		2/Lt. C.A. GREGORY, 15th Essex Regt. Admitted to Hospital — Sick	
	24		Battery attended Brigade Church Parade	
	25		Educational Training.	
	26		do	
	27		do	
	28		Advance Party sent to prepare Billets at NOEUX-LES-MINES.	
	29		Educational Training.	
	30		do	

J.G.B. Capt.
O.C. 177th A.T.M. Bty.

WAR DIARY
INTELLIGENCE SUMMARY.

Army Form C. 2118.

194th Trench Mortar Battery

December 1918.

177 L.T.M. Bty

WAR DIARY
INTELLIGENCE SUMMARY.

Army Form C. 2118.

December 1918

Place	Date	Hour	Summary of Events and Information	Remarks and references to Appendices
SECLIN	Dec 1	11.00	Battery attended Brigade Church Parade.	
"	2	9 & 12.30	Educational Training	
			76374 Pte. HOWTON. O. 2/8th D.L.I. struck off strength. Sick	
"	3	9 & 12.30	Educational Training	
			557755 Cpl JONES. H.A. 15th Essex Regt. admitted to Hospital.	
			257809 L/Cpl JACKSON, J.W. 2/8th D.L.I. do	
"	4	9 & 12.30	Educational Training.	
			407260 Pte CHAPMAN. R. 15th Essex Regt. Admitted to Hospital	
"	5	07.45	Entrained for NOEUX-LES-MINES.	
		14.00	Detrained NOEUX-LES-MINES.	
			Cleaning and Repairing Billets	
			99198 Pte DYER. A. 2/6 D.L.I. Struck off strength. Sick	
NOEUX-LES-MINES	6			
"	7	9 & 12.30	Educational Training	
"	8	10.00	Attended Brigade Church Parade	
			17857 Sergt. G.W. LEE. 11th Somerset L.I. attached to Battery Awarded	
			with M.M. by Divisional Commander.	

177 L.T.M. Bty

WAR DIARY

INTELLIGENCE SUMMARY.

(Erase heading not required.)

Army Form C. 2118.

November 1918

Place	Date	Hour	Summary of Events and Information	Remarks and references to Appendices
NOEUX-LES-MINES	9	09.00 & 12.30	Educational Training. 422071 Pte. TRAVIS. G. 11th Somerset L.I. Admitted to Hospital. Sick.	
"	10	09.00 & 12.30	Educational Training. 55,757 Cpl. JAMES. H.A. 15th Essex Regt. Struck off strength. Sick. 251,607 L/Cpl. JACKSON. J.W. 2/6 D.L.I. do	
"	11	09.00 & 12.30	Educational Training. 407260 Pte. CHAPMAN. R. 15th Essex Regt. Struck off strength. Sick.	
"	12	do	do	
"	13	do	do	
"	14	do		
"	15	11.00	Attended Church Parade. 35/1100 Pte. BROWN. A. Struck off strength. Sick. 420074 Pte. CAMPBELL. W. 11th Somerset L.I. Coal Mines. Struck off strength. Proceed to U.K. for demobilisation. Authy. Demobilisation Circular No. 2.	
"	16	09.00 & 12.30	Educational Training. 47071 Pte. TRAVIS. G. 11th Somerset L.I. Struck off strength. Sick.	
"	17	do	Educational Training.	
"	18	do	do	

Army Form C. 2118.

WAR DIARY
INTELLIGENCE SUMMARY.

(Erase heading not required.)

1/7 A.A. 4th By   November 1918

Instructions regarding War Diaries and Intelligence Summaries are contained in F.S. Regs., Part II. and the Staff Manual respectively. Title pages will be prepared in manuscript.

Place	Date	Hour	Summary of Events and Information	Remarks and references to Appendices
NOEUX-LES-MINES	19	07.00 & 12.30	2/Lieut. C.A. GREGORY. 15th Essex Regt. attached to Battery. Struck off Strength on being evacuated to England. Sick 5/12/18. Educational Training.	
"	20	do	do	
"	21	do	do	
			Promotions:- 252576 L/Cpl RUSHTON. A.S. 15th Essex Regt. } To Lance Corporal Paid 18309 " BENDALL. C.F. 11th Somerset L.I. } with effect from 18290 " TIMBRELL. E.W. do } 27.11.18. 231809 " JACKSON. J.W. 2/6th Durham L.I. } 266253 Pte. BOND. A.C. 11th Somerset L.I. To L/Cpl Paid with effect from 27.11.18. 557575 Cpl. JONES. H.A. 15th Essex Regt. Rejoined Unit from Hospital and is taken on the Strength from 21.12.18.	
"	22		Church Parade. The following N.C.O's and men having been posted to the Battery + complete establishment be taken on the Strength with effect from 22.12.18. 266253 L/Cpl BOND. A.C. 11th Somerset L.I. 78322 Pte. DICKINSON. H.B. do	

Army Form C. 2118.

WAR DIARY
INTELLIGENCE SUMMARY.

(Erase heading not required.)

Instructions regarding War Diaries and Intelligence Summaries are contained in F. S. Regs., Part II. and the Staff Manual respectively. Title pages will be prepared in manuscript.

Place	Date	Hour	Summary of Events and Information	Remarks and references to Appendices
Noeux-Les-Mines			Joiners Out	
	23	07.00 1/2.30	2575576 Cpl RUSHTON A.S. 15th Essex Regt.	
			3571204 Pte ADAM C. do	
			557427 " O'DONOGHUE J. do	
			557267 " BEAMS H.A. do	
			79774 Pte STUDMAN R.G. 2/6 Durham L.I.	
			525442 " HALL L. do	
			99443 " AULT J. do	
			99422 " HEWITT E. do	
			(Authy B.L. X/8/1060 dated 22/12/18)	
			8 Educational Training	
	24	do	do	
	25	do	Xmas Day - Holiday	
	26	do	(Boxing Day) - do	
	27	9.00 1/12.30	Educational Training	
	28	do	do	
	29		Church Parade	
	30	9.00 6/12.30	Educational Training & Bathing	
	31	do	do	

www.ingramcontent.com/pod-product-compliance
Lightning Source LLC
Chambersburg PA
CBHW081445160426
43193CB00013B/2388